Storm at Sea

New Quilts from an Old Favorite

edited by Barbara Smith

American Quilter's Society

P. O. Box 3290 • Paducah, KY 42002-3290

e-mail: AQSquilt@apex.net

Located in Paducah, Kentucky, the American Quilter's Society (AQS) is dedicated to promoting the accomplishments of today's quilters. Through its publications and events, AQS strives to honor today's quiltmakers and their work and to inspire future creativity and innovation in quiltmaking.

Editor: *Barbara Smith*
Book Design/Illustrations: *Lisa M. Clark*
Cover Design: *Michael Buckingham*
Photography: *Charles R. Lynch*

Library of Congress Cataloging-in-Publication Data
Author
        Book title / author
                p.   cm.
        ISBN 1-57432-741-0
        1. Storm at Sea Patterns.   2. Contest.   3. Winning Quilts Featured.   4. Patterns.
5. Techniques.
quilts--United States--History.   I. Title.

                                        Applied for.
                                        CIP

Dedication

This book is dedicated to quiltmakers of all times and all places. Their works inspire and delight us.

Contents

Contents

Preface

This book was developed in conjunction with the annual Museum of the American Quilter's Society (MAQS) contest and exhibit called "New Quilts from Old Favorites." Dedicated to honoring today's quilters, MAQS created this contest to recognize, and share with others, the many fascinating interpretations that can grow out of a single traditional quilt block.

A brief description of the contest is followed by a presentation of the 18 finalists and their quilts, including the five award winners. Full-color photographs of the quilts accompany the quiltmakers' comments, which provide fascinating insights into the creative process. Full-sized templates for the traditional Storm at Sea block, and tips, techniques, and patterns contributed by the contest winners are provided so that you, too, will be able to enjoy making your own Storm at Sea quilt.

It is our hope that this combination of outstanding quilts, patterns, and instructions will inspire as many exciting quilts as the original contest did, adding new contributions to this pattern's continuing tradition.

For information about entering the current year's contest, write to MAQS, PO Box 1540, Paducah, KY 42002-1540.

Storm at Sea

The Contest

Each year, the New Quilts from Old Favorites contest challenges quiltmakers to develop innovative quilts from a different traditional pattern. The theme for 2000 was the Storm at Sea block.

To be entered in the contest, a quilt needed to be recognizable in some way as being related to the Storm at Sea block. The quilt had to be a minimum of 50" in each dimension and was not to exceed 100" in any one dimension, and it had to be quilted. A quilt could only be entered by the person or persons who made it. Many exciting interpretations of the pattern were submitted by quilters from around the world. From these entries, 18 quilts were selected. They are featured in this publication and in a traveling exhibition.

The Storm at Sea Block

Historically, the name "Storm at Sea" has been used for several different blocks, which are better known to us now as Prickly Pear, Flying Dutchman, and Kansas Troubles, among others. The pattern we think of as Storm at Sea starts with a double square-within-a-square block. This simple block is then sashed with an elongated diamond alternated with smaller double square-within-a-square blocks. These simple straight-lined geometric shapes, when combined together and viewed at a distance, produce the illusion of overlapping circles.

From this simple block and sash pattern, our contestants have created many exquisite quilts, some of them quite traditional and others very modern, but all are full of life.

The Winners

Gwenfai Rees Griffiths
Abergele, United Kingdom
SHADES OF THE SARGASSO SEA

Sue Turnquist
Harrisburg, Missouri
RED SKY AT MORNING, SAILOR TAKES WARNING

Inge Mardal and Steen Hougs
Saint-Germain-en-Laye, France
AGAINST THE WIND

Kathy McNeil
Marysville, Washington
ODE TO THE WIND AND WAVES

Nancy Lambert
Pittsburgh, Pennsylvania
PATTERNS II

and the Finalists

Melinda Myrick Brown

Sherri Bain Driver

Marie Karickhoff

Yoshiko Kobayashi

Peggy Luey

Sharon Malec

Claudia Clark Myers

Leslie Rego

Maurine Roy

Judy Sogn

Claire Anne Teagan

Lois Wilson

Adrienne Yorinks

Storm at Sea

First Place

SHADES OF THE SARGASSO SEA

91" x 91", 1999
Cottons, polyester batting
Machine pieced and hand
appliquéd and quilted

Storm at Sea

Gwenfai Rees Griffiths

Abergele, United Kingdom

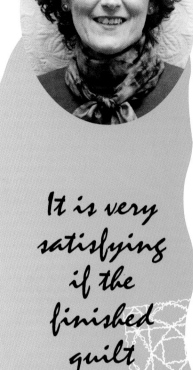

My Quilting

I come from a Welsh-speaking family with deep roots in a very small area of North Wales. I have always been a sewer, knitter, and cross-stitcher...until I discovered quilting. I saw a quilt for the first time in 1992. I had to have one, so I joined a class and was instantly hooked.

I attend many workshops to learn new techniques and pick up new ideas to improve my work. Having no particular style, I use any method needed to achieve the desired effect. My quilts are traditional, but I like to add a new twist, being inspired by others, but never duplicating them.

Initial planning is done in my head. When that picture is clear, I make the paper plans, followed by the most exciting part, the construction. It is very satisfying if the finished quilt matches the picture in my head.

Not a day passes without some involvement in quilting. Evenings at home are spent listening to the TV while I quilt. There aren't enough hours in the day for me, because I always have several ongoing projects at various stages.

My Storm at Sea Quilt

For this quilt, I decided to use a sea theme with the Storm at Sea block as a background. My sister's computer sped up the designing process.

I bought a selection of solid fabrics, shaded from sea blue to green. These were washed and stiffly starched, which helped to prevent the fabrics from shifting during piecing. Looking through books on undersea plants and animals inspired the shapes for the appliqué. The vibrant colors give a floating effect, which stands out against the background.

I applied freezer paper on the backs of the fabrics for the larger pieces, tacking each piece in place before hand sewing it. The smaller pieces were applied by the needle-turn method. Green bias strips link the blocks together, and a curved border design complements the blocks and echoes the appliqué.

The quilting designs are just as important to me as the top's design. Wave patterns were used on either side of the green bias. Coral and sea anemone patterns fill the corners, centers, and borders.

It is very satisfying if the finished quilt matches the picture in my head.

RED SKY AT MORNING,
SAILOR TAKES WARNING

75" x 75", 1999
Cottons, metallic and polyester threac
Machine pieced and reverse
appliquéd, machine appliquéd
and quilted

2 Second Place

Sue Turnquist

Harrisburg, Missouri

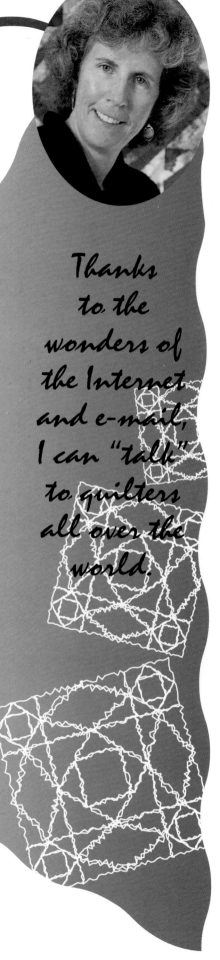

My Quilting

What began as a hobby four years ago has evolved into a passion like no other. I get crabby when I go for more than a day without doing something with fabric.

An acquaintance asked what my creative outlet had been before quilting. My knee-jerk response was "nothing," but then I stopped to ponder. Before quilting, I hadn't had the time or the finances to pursue any latent talent. I stumbled into quilting at a time of personal crises, and I can't help but think there was divine intervention.

Quilting has introduced me to wonderful friends all over the United States. Thanks to the wonders of the Internet and e-mail, I can "talk" to quilters all over the world. I could walk into any quilt shop in the world and strike up a conversation with a total stranger. We pull out photographs, not of our children, but of our quilts, and we have a lovely chat, like two friends who haven't seen each other in years. If my husband happens to be in tow, he will later ask how I know that person. I answer, "I don't know her, but she's a quilter." Enough said!

My Storm at Sea Quilt

I love working with blues, greens, and purples, but for this quilt, I decided to work with the warm half of the color wheel. As might be expected, my fabric stash was a little heavy with cool colors, so I took advantage of a multistate road trip to supplement my supply of rust, gold, and orange fabrics.

I used my computer to help determine color placement and to play with nontraditional settings. The blocks were paper pieced, and a computer program was used to make and print the foundations. I pieced 36 nine-inch blocks and assembled them into a 54" square.

I was less than thrilled with the results until the blocks were set on point. I appliquéd four corner triangles, using both fused and reverse appliqué techniques. The center medallion was free-motion machine quilted with metallic thread on top and clear polyester monofilament in the bobbin. The four corners were couched with a hand-dyed, nubby, wool-blend yarn.

Thanks to the wonders of the Internet and e-mail, I can "talk" to quilters all over the world.

3 *Third Place*

AGAINST THE WIND

50" x 61", 1999
Cottons
Machine pieced and quilted,
hand appliquéd

Storm at Sea

Inge Mardal & Steen Hougs

Saint-Germain-en-Laye, France

Our Quilting

We are Danish in origin and have, for professional reasons, lived in Germany, the United States, Canada, and now France. Regarding the artistic side of our lives, it could be said that we are self-taught and have individually explored various kinds of needle-work (Inge) and painting (Steen) for a long time, but in recent years, these activities have developed into several joint projects.

The design stage is important for us, and we rarely use traditional blocks. One could say that we have a painterly approach, though we normally use ordinary fabrics rather than dyed or painted ones.

In 1997, we decided to share our works with a larger audience, and for this we chose internationally recognized exhibitions. It has turned out to be a very challenging, but also very inspiring, experience.

Fabric is a fascinating medium. The inherent multitude of possibilities for expressing ideas, feelings, surfaces, and shapes invites continued exploration. We have just begun.

Our Storm at Sea Quilt

We love spending our vacations at the seaside. Maybe it is because of our Danish origin, where one never is more than 35 miles away from the sea. Maybe it is because we love watching birds, breathing fresh air, observing the ever-changing seascape, and sensing the impressive forces of the waves and the wind…maybe it's a blend of all those factors. Adding to this is our support for the philosophy behind the MAQS New Quilts from an Old Favorite contest, which bridges the categories of traditional and contemporary quiltmaking.

In AGAINST THE WIND, we particularly like the firm and uncomplicated design. It supports well the rendering of the monumentality of a stormy sea and the persisting calmness with which the gloomy sky seems to build up from the horizon.

Through its contrasting elegance and lightness, the gull, Larus Canus, as it glides against the wind, contrasts with the rough sea. In Danish, this bird is called Storm Gull – in this case, a very appropriate name.

In Danish, this bird is called storm gull – in this case, a very appropriate name.

4 Fourth Place

ODE TO THE WIND AND WAVES

70" x 90", 1999
Cottons, iridescent organza,
rayon and metallic threads
Machine pieced, appliquéd,
and embroidered

Kathy McNeil

Marysville, Washington

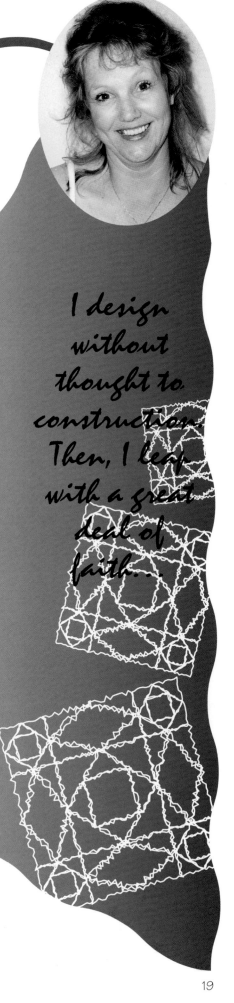

My Quilting

I started quilting three and a half years ago when my oldest daughter requested a quilt for her college room. At the same time, I was dabbling in painting a huge mural on all four of my bedroom walls.

Painting was an attempt to return to something I had loved as a child. Parenting four children and working full time had not left a lot of time for me. I was afraid that, once I gave way to the seductive call of personal time, I would be so absorbed that the family would riot.

Instead, I have found that children come and do homework on the cutting table next to the sewing machine. They even bring their friends to see the current project, and my loyal and supportive husband assumed many of the household and parenting chores.

My Storm at Sea Quilt

In January 1999, my husband nearly drowned sea-kayaking at night in a storm. This quilt is the song from my heart for his safe return.

In making my quilt, I used a hoop for stabilizing. I spent many, many hours in thread play, doodling across the wave. The notes are machine embroidered, and the waves are just random shapes layered over each other on the design wall until the effect was pleasing.

During my design time, the house could burn down and I might not notice. I design without thought to construction. Then, I leap with a great deal of faith, poring through my many quilting books to find a technique that can best translate the image into fabric.

I project my drawing to a size I like and trace it on a wall covered in freezer paper. As the pieces are made, they are placed under a tracing-paper copy of the design to ensure proper placement before sewing them together. From there, I use foundation paper piecing, appliqué, machine embroidery, or whatever technique is most suited to bringing forth the design.

I design without thought to construction. Then, I leap with a great deal of faith...

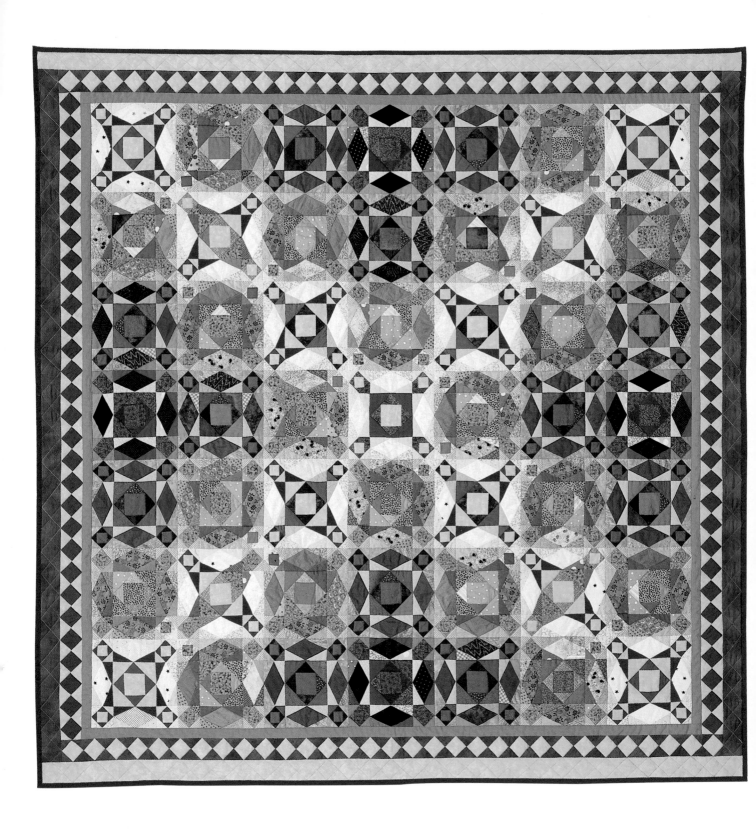

5 Fifth Place

PATTERNS II

66" x 66", 1999
Cotton fabrics, invisible thread
Machine foundation
paper pieced

Storm at Sea

Nancy Lambert

Pittsburgh, Pennsylvania

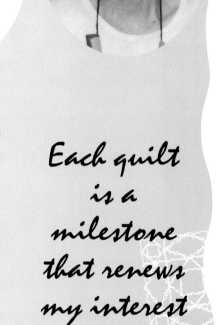

My Quilting

My first quilt was a sampler, made more than 10 years ago. It was made with lap-quilting techniques. Over the years, my quilting evolved from purely traditional to more artistic.

I enjoy developing designs for new quilts, taking a concept and trying to turn it into a visually pleasing piece. Often, it is so surprising to see how an idea can be translated into fabric and thread.

I also enjoy machine quilting and would like to quilt more, if time allowed. I always try to keep at least one project going at all times. I love to work with fabric, color, and design. These are very relaxing and stimulating to me. I'm not able to make and finish many quilts, so each one is a milestone that renews my interest in making the next one.

My Storm at Sea Quilt

PATTERNS II is made from a Storm at Sea block in which the sashing is repeated. First, I made a drawing of all the blocks in the quilt. The drawing was divided horizontally, vertically, and diagonally.

Next, I colored the drawing. The blocks along the diagonals were colored to stand out, creating another design element. The coloration in each of the quarter sections is symmetrical and identical.

In choosing fabrics, I wanted to vary the color gradations between the blocks without using dyed fabric, which would have the perfectly correct hues. I introduced a variety of small prints to add interest. So, from a distance, each color looks like a solid, but if you are close, you can see the subtle variations.

I wanted the quilt to be light, airy, and have a cheerful attitude. If I were to make the quilt again, I might try having the colors blend more gradually for a softer overall appearance.

Each quilt is a milestone that renews my interest in making the next one.

Finalist

GIFTS FROM THE SEA

95" x 95", 1997
Cottons, nylon thread
Hand and machine pieced,
machine quilted, hand appliquéd

Storm at Sea

Melinda Myrick Brown

Washington, DC

My Quilting

Sewing has been a part of my life for as long as I can remember. At age 8, I started making doll clothes by hand and moved from there to making my first garment on a toy sewing machine. By junior high, I was making most of my wardrobe on my mother's sewing machine.

My first quilting attempt was in 1974. I hand pieced half of the Log Cabin blocks for a full-sized quilt for my daughter. It took me two years to finish machine piecing the top. I set out to machine quilt it, knowing nothing about walking feet or basting. After a few attempts, the quilt was placed in a brown paper bag until it was hand quilted by a local quilting group.

Eventually, I decided to make a new attempt at machine quilting. A class with Harriet Hargrave got me over that hump and left me free to be creative. I have now developed my own style, characterized by the use of many different fabrics and by heavy quilting.

I have become fond of curved piecing and have done a lot of hand piecing. Since retiring in 1998, I am now able to devote most of my time to quilting.

My Storm at Sea Quilt

GIFTS FROM THE SEA started as pieced sea urchins, designed in a class with Ruth McDowell. The class, called Designing from Nature, was a real stretch for me. I had never counted drawing among my talents. It was such a freeing experience to do something I had thought was beyond my abilities. I made a dozen sea urchins, with no idea of what to do with them. (Sea urchin pattern, pages 62–64.)

Storm at Sea had always been a favorite pattern of mine, but the colors normally used weren't in my palette. I suddenly realized that, by adding the sea urchins to a Storm at Sea, I could get back to familiar geometric lines and that, with my earth-toned sea urchins, the sea colors would be comfortable for me.

The quilt contains three sizes of Storm at Sea blocks: 6", 12", and 24". (Full-size patterns, pages 48–55.) A computer quilt-design program was helpful in making the templates in each of the required sizes. I created 16 of the smallest block and 12 each of the two larger sizes. The largest block had to be modified to insert the sea urchin. I hand drafted the template for fitting the sea urchin into the largest square in the largest block.

It was such a freeing experience to do something I had thought was beyond my abilities.

Finalist

STORM WARNING

58" x 58", 1999
Hand-dyed cotton, ikats, poly-
ester-cotton blend chambray
Hand and machine pieced,
machine quilted

Sherri Bain Driver

Englewood, Colorado

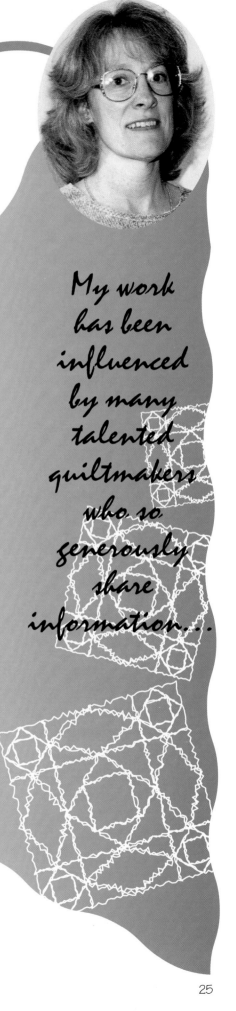

My Quilting

I've always loved fabrics, sewing, and all kinds of needlework, but my obsession with quilting began in 1987 when I joined a quilting group as a way to meet friends after a move. I had no idea how important quiltmaking and quilting friends would become in my life.

My first quilts were traditional and often made from patterns. As my confidence grew, I began to design quilts and started teaching. Customers liked the designs, so writing patterns and giving lectures and workshops soon followed. Now, I'm working as an editor for a quilting magazine — truly a dream job!

I love every bit of the quiltmaking process from the first glimmer of a new design idea to the last stitch of the binding. It's exciting to see a final product that began as a doodle. I like to enter shows and contests, because a deadline helps me finish a project.

My work has been influenced by many talented quiltmakers, who so generously share information in classes, books, and lectures.

My Storm at Sea Quilt

I am intrigued by straight-seamed quilts that create the illusion of circles. I've made several quilts using the triangles that form these pseudo curves and "long-legged stars" and thought it would be fun to make a Storm at Sea quilt to enter in the MAQS contest. I also wanted to dip into my stash of ikat fabrics.

The design for STORM WARNING was begun by making a computer drawing of a square quilt consisting of 25 Storm at Sea blocks. I printed out several copies and colored them to see what shapes could be found that would look interesting when cut from ikats. The final design had many odd angles, so some of the seams needed to be sewn by hand to keep the points sharp.

I usually have several projects going at the same time, some in the design phase, some being pieced, and at least one in the quilting stage. My sewing room is arranged so that, when sitting at the sewing machine, I face my design wall. Short breaks from machine quilting are then used to cut pieces for a new quilt, arranging and auditioning fabrics on the design wall.

My work has been influenced by many talented quiltmakers who so generously share information...

MER DES SARGASSES

65" x 81", 1997
Cottons
Machine pieced and quilted

26

Storm at Sea

Marie Karickhoff

South Lyon, Michigan

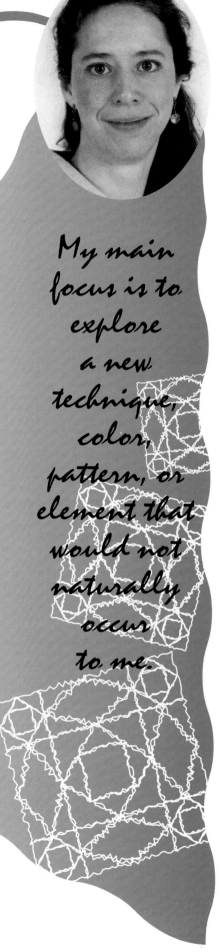

My Quilting

In the 1970s, I saw a picture of an Ocean Waves quilt that was simply awesome, so I pledged to learn more about quilting. In 1994, I joined a quilting guild, more to get away from the house and kids for an evening than to gain knowledge, but nevertheless, my love of quilting grew. That summer, I made an "if-you-make-it-they-will-come" quilt. Shortly after finishing it, I became pregnant with our third child for whom it was intended.

Now, I have many projects dancing in my head. Some will have to simmer on the back burner for years, while others will be born in three days. My main focus is to explore a new technique, color, pattern, or element that would not naturally occur to me.

I am self-taught and enjoy drafting the most. I use graph paper, pencil, ruler, and my daughter's felt markers for my initial drafts. Computer software has allowed me to master quickly and efficiently my final designs. Unknown to most people, I frequently incorporate symbols and counting games in my quilts.

My Storm at Sea Quilt

MER DES SARGASSES is a gift to my mother, Marie Gratton. Nothing better than a quilt could express my love and gratitude to her. The greens and browns of the quilt closely portray the textures and colors of sargassum, a brownish alga or gulf weed. Massive expanses of these weeds create a relatively still sea in the Atlantic Ocean, known as the Sargasso Sea or, in French, Mer des Sargasses.

I used computer software to design the quilt. The center consists of traditional Storm at Sea blocks. However, the blocks in the perimeter have been changed by removing the center square and two adjacent corner triangles. They were replaced with a dark and a light strip to create an airy inner edge to the sash. A solid, light border frames the outer sash. Notice how the top and bottom borders do not mirror each other. It's no accident.

The metamorphosis of the outermost sash into a beaded border creates the endless movement within the quilt's center.

My main focus is to explore a new technique, color, pattern, or element that would not naturally occur to me.

ANCIENT MIRROR CAME FROM
ACROSS THE SEA

60¼" x 60¼", 1999
Commercial fabrics,
hand-dyed fabrics
Machine foundation paper
pieced and hand quilted

Finalist

Yoshiko Kobayashi

Osaka, Japan

My Quilting

About 11 years ago, I became involved in quiltmaking after being inspired by a quilt exhibition in Nagoya, Japan. After studying quiltmaking for four years, I moved to Osaka, and continued quiltmaking by self-teaching.

After attending a workshop by Nancy Crow in Osaka, I have been trying some machine piecing. Now, my elderly mother lives alone near my house and needs my help for her daily life, so it is hard to find many hours for making quilts. Using a sewing machine, therefore, is indispensable for my quiltmaking, and the machine enables me to enter contests with deadlines.

I'm honored to have three quilts that have been finalists in MAQS contests. The first quilt was WWW NAVIGATOR'S COMPASS in the Mariner's Compass Quilt Contest, and the second was the EARLY SPRING WOOD in the Kaleidoscope Quilt Contest. I would like to see if I can handle an even greater challenge next time.

My Storm at Sea Quilt

My quilt, ANCIENT MIRROR CAME FROM ACROSS THE SEA, shows an ancient bronze mirror, such as found in old tombs. Most of these mirrors have beautiful engraved designs on the back that consist of flowers, leaves, fruits, the four god beasts, and the like.

My daughter, who is 15 years old, likes history, and she is also interested in old things, especially the four god beasts. So, I happened to think of this quilt design from a conversation with my daughter.

The four god beasts are imaginary creatures from ancient China, and they consist of Seiryu, a blue dragon from the east; Suzaku, a red phoenix from the south; Byakko, a white tiger from the west; and Genbu, the snake-tortoise from the north. I quilted the dragon and phoenix on the mirror in my quilt. (Dragon and phoenix quilting patterns, pages 75–76.)

I also quilted 28 constellations with red and gold thread on my quilt. The constellations were found on the wall of an ancient tomb. They were brought to Japan from China across the Japan Sea in ancient times.

The four god beasts are imaginary creatures from ancient China....

REQUIEM AT SEA

50" x 50", 1998
Commercial and
hand-dyed cottons
Machine pieced and quilted

Finalist

Storm at Sea

Peggy Luey
Charlotte, North Carolina

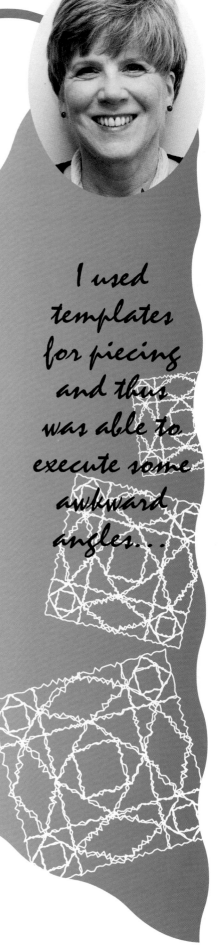

My Quilting

My interest in quilting began when the mother of one of my piano students brought a quilt she was working on to the lessons. I remember thinking how beautiful the designs and colors were, and what love she put into her stitches. That was about 15 years ago, but I was not able to begin my own foray into the quilt world until 1990. At that time, my husband was transferred, and I gave up my piano business.

I put my whole heart into learning the necessary quilting skills. I have attended many classes. I love to read all the quilting magazines and have that well-known obsession for collecting, and now dyeing, fabric. Designing and sewing quilts has become the most important part of my life, after my family. A day without quilting is like a day without sunshine!

My work is going in two directions at the present time. One is a rather free improvisational style of working without a preset design, just letting the fabric lead me. The other is drafting rather complex designs on paper, full-sized, and using templates.

My Storm at Sea Quilt

REQUIEM AT SEA was made as a tribute to those who lost their lives in the TWA Flight 800 crash off Long Island in 1996. The quilt design consists of sixteen 12" Storm at Sea blocks with a 48" transparent block superimposed over the whole quilt.

For the most part, I used templates for piecing (squares and right triangles excluded) and thus was able to execute some awkward angles and very small pieces that were the result of the overlaid design. Fabrics are both commercial and hand-dyed and were chosen with the goal of achieving an effective transparency.

This quilt was a special challenge to me. I have made other quilts with transparencies but never one where the larger overlying motif did not fall on the seam lines.

All in all, I am happy with the final result. There is one piece I wish I could take out and do over, but that will be my secret!

I used templates for piecing and thus was able to execute some awkward angles. . .

Finalist

WHALE OF A STORM

51½" x 51½", 1999
Cotton batiks, hand-dyed and hand
painted cottons, dyed cheesecloth
Machine pieced, appliquéd, and quilte

Storm at Sea

Sharon Malec

West Chicago, Illinois

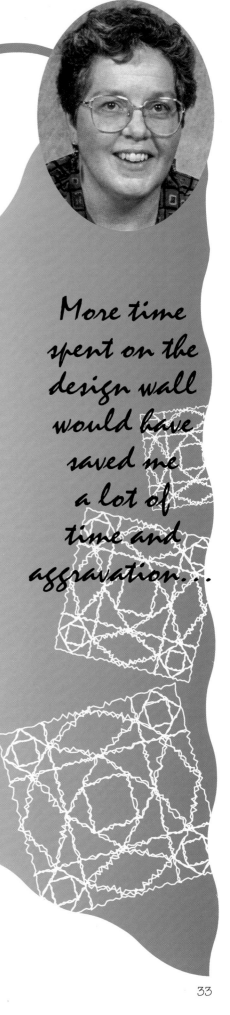

My Quilting

I began quilting about eight years ago after selling a craft business. I was intrigued by the colors and designs used in traditional quilts and had intended to remain a traditional quilter. I wasn't interested in contemporary art quilts until I saw Cynthia England's PIECE AND QUIET. I knew then that I wanted to make pictorial quilts.

The next several years were spent exploring construction methods and developing a method of freestanding appliqué. I enjoy sharing what I have learned with other quilters by teaching at local quilt shops and guilds and by developing my own line of quilt patterns.

Although the focus of my work is pictorial art quilts, I still make one hand-pieced traditional quilt each year as a donation to a convalescent center. The quilt is raffled as a fund-raiser.

To date, I have made more than 200 quilts and can't wait to get started on the next project. I often work on two to six projects at one time.

My Storm at Sea Quilt

The perimeter of the quilt consists of 16" machine-pieced Storm at Sea blocks in gradated colors to reflect the sky and water. The whale's tail is machine appliquéd. The whale was drawn on paper, enlarged on a photocopier, and then traced on freezer paper. The freezer paper pieces served as templates for the appliqué. (Whale pattern, pages 78–80.)

I liked the image of a whale splashing down but wasn't sure how to execute the water running off the tail. Then I watched an IMAX film on whales and saw some real whales in British Columbia.

When all the blocks were assembled, the whale did not stand out as I had hoped. A friend suggested I change the sky fabric directly above the whale and this led to completely rebuilding most of the blocks to arrive at the finished color scheme. More time spent on the design wall would have saved me a lot of time and aggravation rebuilding all the blocks.

The quilt is embellished with dyed cheesecloth and fabric paint, and it is machine free-motion quilted.

More time spent on the design wall would have saved me a lot of time and aggravation. . . .

Kosovo – A World in Flames

60" x 80", 1999
Cottons, rayon thread
Machine pieced, quilted, and
embroidered; photo transfers;
hand bound

Finalist

Claudia Clark Myers

Duluth, Minnesota

My Quilting

My Grandma Clark taught me to embroider daisies and fancy ladies on pillowcases. I watched my Grandma De Temple as she ran the old Singer treadle, making clothes for my dolls, while my mom made most of our clothes. For 25 years, I designed and made costumes and now spend my retirement quilting with my daughter. The art and craft of sewing has had a huge impact on several generations of women in my family. From doll clothes and little girls' dresses to opera headpieces and "arty" quilts, sewing has given us all a means of self-expression, of earning respect, of earning a living.

I will forever be grateful to the women in my life who taught me to sew, even the junior-high home economics teacher who flunked me because I refused to baste my apron project. My mother had long before taught me to sew, with no basting, and I certainly wasn't going to start basting aprons. For the last nine years, I have been learning to quilt. Ironically, one of the first things I learned was how to baste a quilt.

My Storm at Sea Quilt

A clipping from *The Smithsonian* magazine was the driving force for this quilt. It is a black and white photo of a group of perhaps 20 women refugees, clustered in the rubble of their city. I was very moved by the photographed and hoped that someday I could make a quilt to honor their bravery.

When I began working on my entry in the MAQS Storm at Sea challenge, I considered creating a quilt based on the sinking of the Edmund Fitzgerald. Because I live on Lake Superior and remember when that tragic event occurred, it seemed a natural choice.

I drafted 11 different rectangular Storm at Sea background blocks and made many copies of each. However, as I was rearranging my longest blocks on the design wall, I noticed that, done in the right fabrics, these blocks could look like flames. What better background for my embattled refugees? So, I switched ideas, concentrating on fire rather than water.

I will forever be grateful to the women in my life who taught me to sew.

The refugees were drawn from a photo titled, "The Wives and Mothers of Those Killed in Srebrenica, Bosnia, 1996," published in *The Graves: Srebrenica and Vukovar*, written by Eric Stover and photographed by Gilles Peress. Courtesy Magnum Photos in New York City.

Finalist

JUBILATION

65" x 65"
Cottons, metallic threads
Machine pieced and quilted

Storm at Sea

Leslie Rego
Sun Valley, Idaho

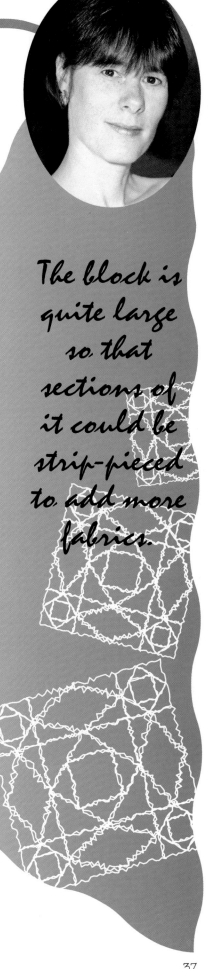

My Quilting

For my first quilt in 1982, I selected the pattern with the most templates. Of course, I quickly became bogged down. For my next quilt, according to the fashion of the day, I chose two colors and white muslin, which was incredibly boring.

I decided to try to make my quilts more interesting, so I bought 30 different half-yard pieces of peach and light orange. The results were exciting, and for the first time, I enjoyed quiltmaking.

For my palette, I now have around 1,500 pieces of fabric, all sorted according to color and shade. In 1993, I entered a quilt in my first juried show, the American Quilter's Society Show in Paducah, Kentucky, and was thrilled to be accepted. To my further delight, the quilt won third place in the theme category.

I have begun to play with dyeing and painting. I easily use 50 or more fabrics in a piece and am always intrigued by how so many different fabrics fit together. I primarily work with unlikely color combinations and asymmetrical designs.

My Storm at Sea Quilt

I designed JUBILATION when my son Brennan was quite sick. I promised him this quilt if he would go without complaining to the doctor's office for tests. I made the quilt as "happy" as I could, thus, all the polka dots and bright colors. Brennan was very brave and, in due course, he got well.

The block is quite large, 17" x 17", so that sections of it could be strip-pieced to add more fabrics. All the seams are pieced in straight lines but, through their placement, an optical illusion of curves results.

I decided to add the red areas to give a feeling of tension and movement across the quilt face. The blue fabric in the border areas has a lighter edge, which was placed against the body of the quilt, and a darker edge, which became one of the outside borders. The four corners of the blue fabric were mitered so the light areas would run diagonally across the border.

The challenge was getting all the bright fabrics to work together and still have rest areas for the eye. That is why I included the blue-gray and hand-dyed fabrics around the center diamond.

The block is quite large so that sections of it could be strip-pieced to add more fabrics.

Finalist

AUTUMN LEAVES

57" x 56", 1997
Cottons, rayon thread
Machine pieced, quilted,
and embroidered

Storm at Sea

Maurine Roy

Edmonds, Washington

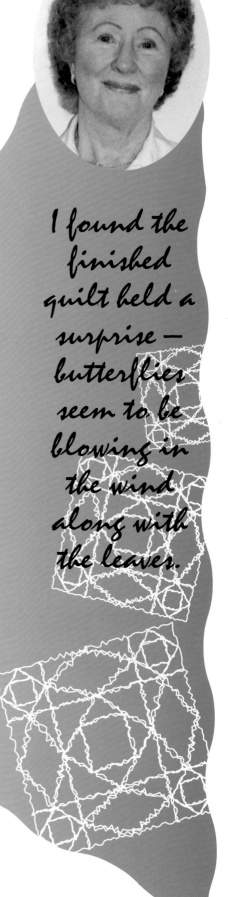

My Quilting

I have been quilting since 1990 and have finished more than 141 quilts, from wall- to king-size. Some are hand quilted, but most are machine quilted. I made six quilts that were color studies. This series called "My Precious Gems" included ruby, topaz, sapphire, emerald, pearl, and amethyst.

Many of my quilts reflect my experiences and feelings. I have made quite a few "therapy" quilts, including AUTUMN LEAVES. Somehow, working with the texture and color of fabric helps to release and soothe emotions.

I enjoy the challenge of trying new ideas and new concepts in quilt design. A lot of my inspiration comes from the wonderful fabrics that are available, and I have started dyeing my own. Quilting is an amazing art form. Once having stepped into that world, I found there are no limitations placed on my creativity or my depth of feelings.

My Storm at Sea Quilt

Storm at Sea has always been one of my favorite patterns, but I never found time to make it. Then I discovered a wonderful batik fabric with leaves that seemed to fade in and out. My theme for the quilt was "When Autumn Leaves Start to Fall." Then I recalled the Storm at Sea pattern and started playing around with the idea of distorting the block in several ways to see what different kinds of movement were possible.

I used two color gradations, a yellow to orange-red gradation and a fuchsia to dark blue. I colored in the gradations on my paper pattern, and as each block was made, it was placed on my work wall. It was quite a challenge to piece.

I used hand-dyed fabrics for the gradations. I liked the soft sueded look of them. I machine embroidered the leaves with rayon thread. They were sewn on the quilt to give a three-dimensional effect. I found the finished quilt held a surprise — butterflies seem to be blowing in the wind along with the leaves.

> *I found the finished quilt held a surprise — butterflies seem to be blowing in the wind along with the leaves.*

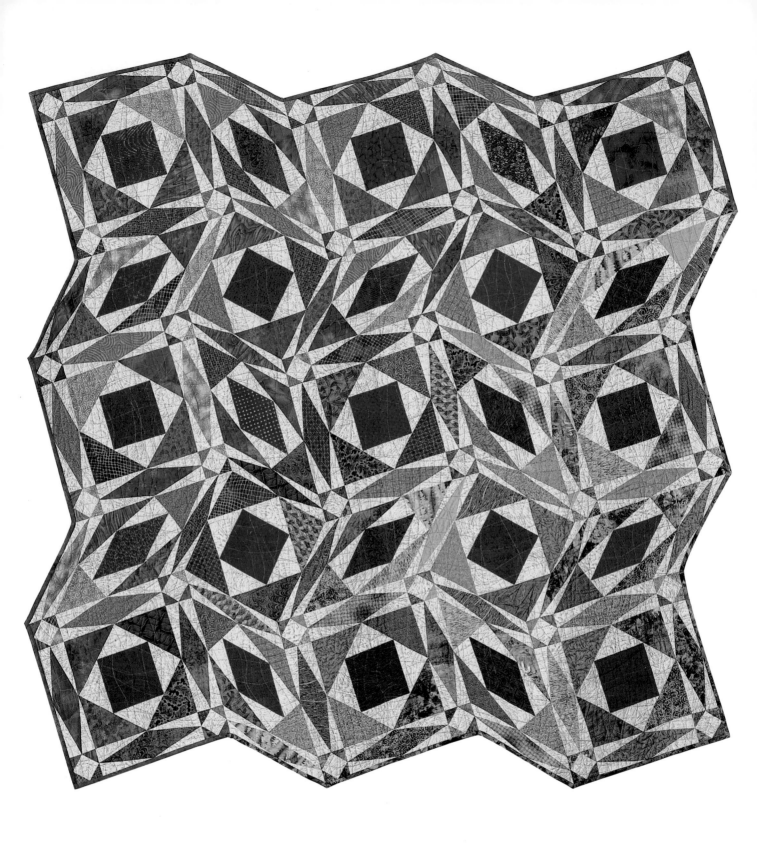

STORM AT…GULP…SEASICK

52" x 52", 1999
Cottons, rayon thread
Machine pieced and quilted

Finalist

Storm at Sea

Judy Sogn
Seattle, Washington

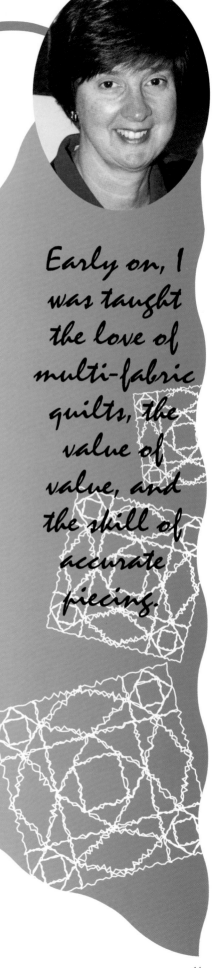

My Quilting

I became a quilter almost reluctantly, trying a variety of new handwork techniques to make gifts for friends and family. Eventually, I realized I could probably make a quilt with all my new skills. I made a lap-sized sampler quilt and was hooked.

Early on, I was taught the love of multi-fabric quilts, the value of value, and the skill of accurate piecing. Today, I enjoy using my computer to design quilts and to make decorative quilt labels with clip art and fancy fonts. Quilting is a wonderful medium because I can make something original even though I'm not good at drawing or painting.

Currently, I am using foundation paper piecing. I am amazed at the intricate pictorial designs possible with this technique. Another interest is Hawaiian quilts. I have completed two wall quilts based on purchased patterns and hope to design my own. After attending a recent lecture on Welsh quilts, I am looking forward to designing and quilting a whole-cloth quilt incorporating designs based on the Welsh traditions.

My Storm at Sea Quilt

Lately, I have been experimenting with jagged-edge quilts. For my Storm at Sea quilt, I used a set of alternating squares and diamonds to achieve a very jagged edge. The uneven edge reminded me of the surface of a storm-tossed sea, thus the title. I then decided to continue with the seasick theme and used yellow greens to enhance the effect. Rather than make the entire quilt of these often unpopular colors, I chose to transition from a beautiful peaceful turquoise sea to the stomach-churning colors of the lower right corner.

I machine quilted undulating wavy lines all over the surface of the quilt in rayon thread matching the colors of the fabrics. I had fun with the back of this quilt, using a variation of the Snail's Trail block to form waves. A small paper-pieced sailboat is caught in the heart of a wave.

If I were to change something in this quilt, I might make the "seasick" area of the quilt smaller and increase the size of the transition area. On the whole though, I'm very pleased with the way it turned out.

Early on, I was taught the love of multi-fabric quilts, the value of value, and the skill of accurate piecing.

Storm at Sea

Finalist

Tumbling Seas

51" x 60", 1999
Commercial cotton batiks, hand-
dyed and painted cottons
Machine foundation pieced
and quilted

Claire Anne Teagan

Highland, Michigan

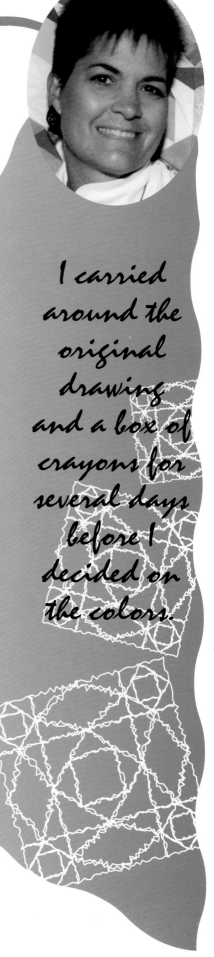

My Quilting

My mother taught me to sew at age 7, and I spent all my allowance on material. In 1975 or 1976, I made my first quilt, a Log Cabin, and gave it to my brother for high school graduation. I made a couple of quilts in college, but I was still involved in my earlier interests of sewing, knitting, and ceramic sculpture.

My first quilting instruction came from a PBS series on TV. From there, I started taking classes at quilt shops. Like most beginners, every room and couch in the house had a quilt or three on it. Finding a quilt guild gave me the support, techniques, and friendly critics that I needed to really improve. Some of my best work has come from challenges or group showings.

Most of my pieces are appliquéd and incorporate painted and dyed fabrics and free-motion machine embroidery. Many of the quilts have come from family photographs.

My Storm at Sea Quilt

The fabrics used in TUMBLING SEAS are mostly batiks, but the quilt also contains some commercial fabrics and my hand-dyed and painted ones. I also over-dyed or painted some of the commercial fabrics.

A computer quilt-design program was used to turn the Storm at Sea block into a 60° diamond and to place the diamonds in a tumbling-block setting.

I carried around the original drawing (page 90) and a box of crayons for several days before deciding on the colors. I tried different coloring ideas while waiting for my kids at school. My daughter even colored a few for me.

The quilt, which contains 1,444 pieces, is made of three differently colored blocks. The six outer diamonds have dark-blue backgrounds. Three of the center diamonds have medium-blue backgrounds, and three have light blue. I used a color diagram for sewing the different diamonds. The four outer triangles are batiks.

> I carried around the original drawing and a box of crayons for several days before I decided on the colors.

Finalist

LOST IN THE STARS

74" x 92", 1996
Cottons
Hand pieced and appliquéd

Storm at Sea

Lois Wilson
West Union, Ohio

My Quilting

I began quilting in the early 1980s. I was working for an interior designer, and one of the displays in the shop included an antique cradle which needed a small quilt to show it off properly. I knew nothing about quilting but decided to attempt it anyway. I selected a Mother Goose pattern because I knew how to appliqué, a skill I had learned in elementary school. When the little quilt was finished, the appliqué was all right, but the quilting was terrible. However, from a distance it looked fine in the cradle. I was proud of it and was determined to learn to quilt.

In 1987, I enrolled in a beginning quilting and appliqué class. The teacher encouraged me to show my quilts and enter contests. One of the quilts I had made for my son's room won the Best Workmanship Award at The Dairy Barn in Athens, Ohio, in 1988, and was shown at the AQS show in 1989.

I continued to enter shows and received several awards. All of these quilts were mainly appliqué, so I am particularly delighted that my LOST IN THE STARS quilt has been accepted for the Storm at Sea exhibit.

My Storm at Sea Quilt

Although I mostly do hand-appliquéd quilts, I'm always looking at patchwork patterns and admiring the intricate designs. I began this hand-pieced quilt in March 1992 and finished it in August 1996. I found that the project was so portable, a pleasurable way to pass the time. I could work on the blocks while I had to wait for appointments.

Periodically, I would open the box where I stored the blocks and count them to see how many more I would need. Then each block I pulled out of the storage box would bring memories of its construction. When I finally had all the blocks done and was putting them up on my flannel wall, I found that I became totally immersed in arranging the stars. That is when I named it LOST IN THE STARS.

Once I got all the blocks sewed together, I had to decide on a border. It was then that I decided to place some clusters of stars that I had drawn free-hand on the deep-navy border, hopefully to emphasize the Stars at Sea pattern. I even quilted stars in the border. I used the reverse side of the navy-blue border to separate those perfect stars from the free-hand drawn ones and also used the reverse side to bind the quilt. I have found that often the reverse side of a fabric complements the right side, and I have no problems whatever with using both sides of a fabric.

> I found that the project was so portable, a pleasurable way to pass the time.

Finalist

DUCKING THE STORM

50" x 55", 1999
Vintage flannel premiums,
ca. 1910, cottons, rayon blends
Machine pieced, appliquéd,
and quilted

Adrienne Yorinks

North Salem, New York

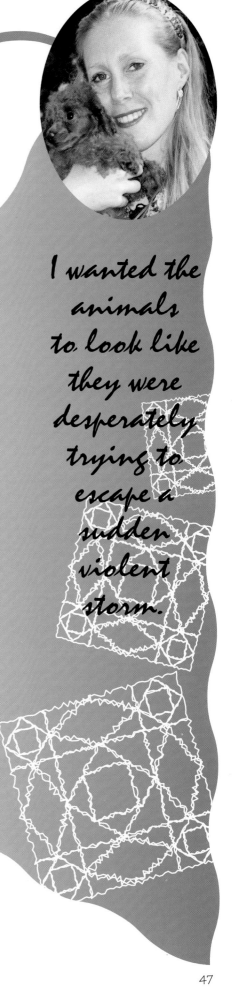

My Quilting

I was born on Staten Island, New York, but I now live in upstate New York with my husband, Arthur, and our six dogs: three border collies and three red poodles.

I am a fabric artist who likes to blend the traditional and the modern and try to work in many different styles and sizes. My commissioned work ranges from a 10' x 8½' nine-panel piece, commemorating the 150th anniversary of the City University of New York, to a series of twenty-five 10" x 8" pieces illustrating Eugene O'Neill's book, *The Last Will and Testament of an Extremely Distinguished Dog.*

My own work tends to be large, such as a 79" x 71" piece celebrating the birth of women's suffrage in America. The quilt recently came back from a national tour through Quilt National.

I am quite excited by having designed a fabric line for Hi-Fashion Fabrics, which will debut this spring, and I recently completed a commission from the AFL-CIO to highlight its commitment to civil rights in the United States.

My Storm at Sea Quilt

I wanted to make a Storm at Sea quilt that was unique, yet still echoed the original pattern, and I wanted to challenge myself to use the vintage tobacco-company premiums I had purchased. The premiums are the scurrying creatures.

As I looked at Storm at Sea quilts, I began to see the essence of the pattern and how I could manipulate it. What struck me most was the movement. At times, it almost looked dizzying. Black, white, and gray stripes created the motion I wanted in Ducking the Storm.

The diagonal lines were also fascinating. I loved the feeling of the sharp diagonals within the moving piece. The color yellow created the right thrust.

The third aspect I noticed was the tight vertical rows of blocks. When I placed the vintage animals in their spots, they began to look like they were scurrying. I enhanced the feeling by facing them so they appeared to be running off the quilt. I wanted the animals to look like they were desperately trying to escape a sudden violent storm.

I wanted the animals to look like they were desperately trying to escape a sudden violent storm.

Storm at Sea Patterns

Block Patterns

Included in this section are full-sized templates for traditional Storm at Sea blocks in six sizes. Select the size most appropriate for your project plans.

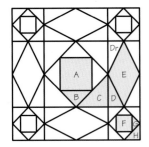

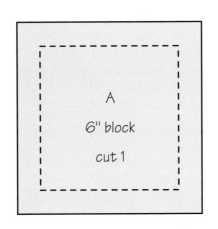

A
6" block
cut 1

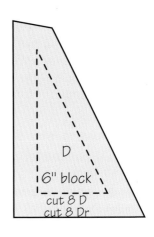

D
6" block
cut 8 D
cut 8 Dr

B
6" block
cut 4

F
6" block
cut 4

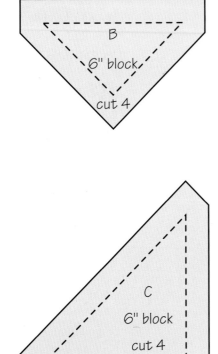

C
6" block
cut 4

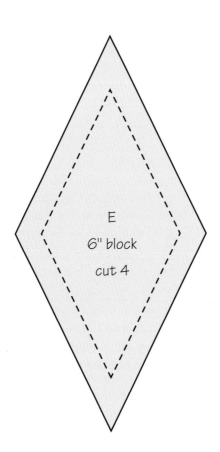

E
6" block
cut 4

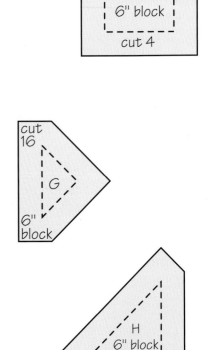

cut 16

G
6" block

H
6" block
cut 16

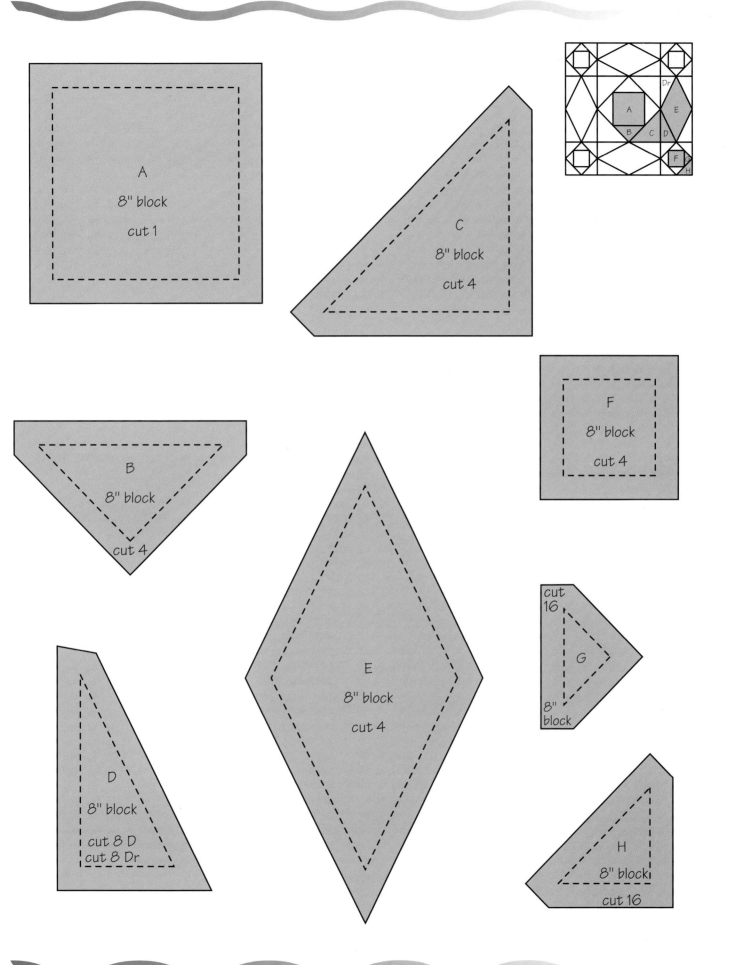

A

8" block

cut 1

C

8" block

cut 4

Dr

A

E

B

C

D

F

G

H

B

8" block

cut 4

F

8" block

cut 4

D

8" block

cut 8 D
cut 8 Dr

E

8" block

cut 4

cut
16

G

8"
block

H

8" block

cut 16

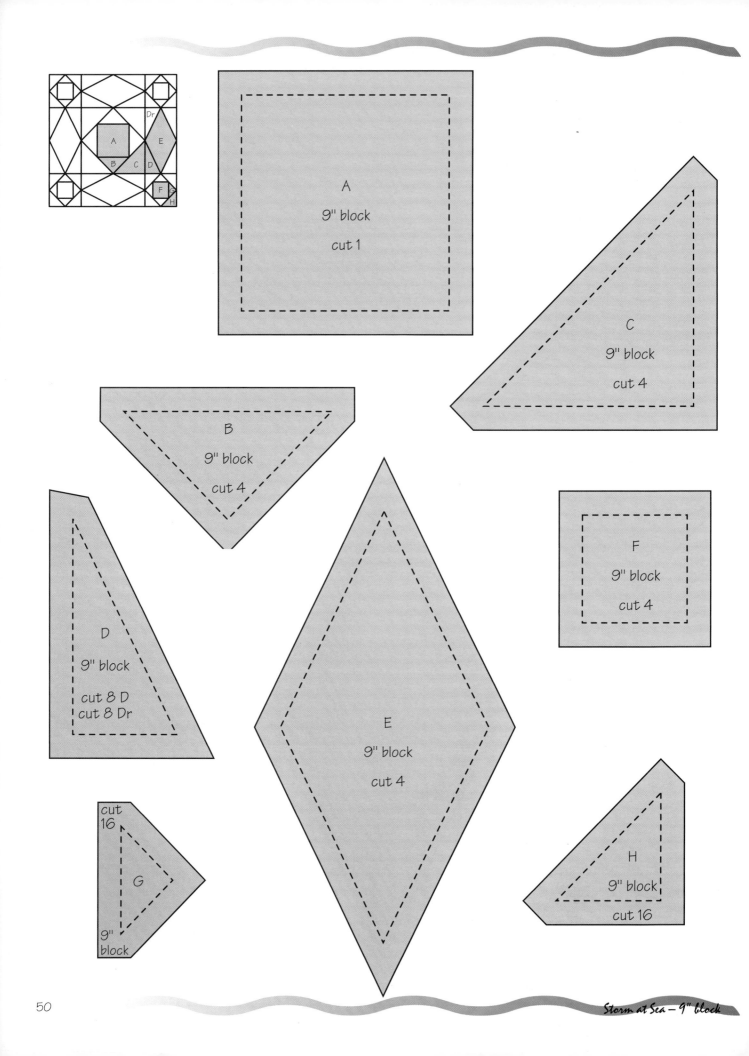

A

9" block

cut 1

C

9" block

cut 4

B

9" block

cut 4

F

9" block

cut 4

D

9" block

cut 8 D
cut 8 Dr

E

9" block

cut 4

cut
16

G

9" block

H

9" block

cut 16

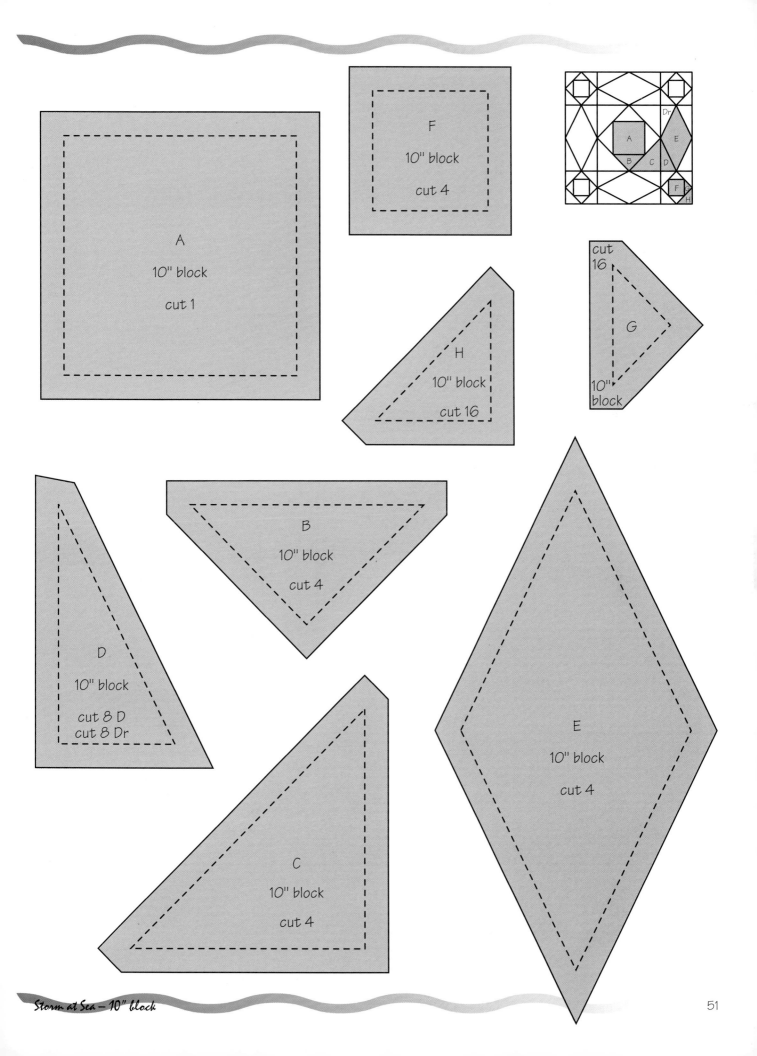

F
10" block
cut 4

A
10" block
cut 1

cut 16

G
10"
block

H
10" block
cut 16

B
10" block
cut 4

D
10" block

cut 8 D
cut 8 Dr

E
10" block
cut 4

C
10" block
cut 4

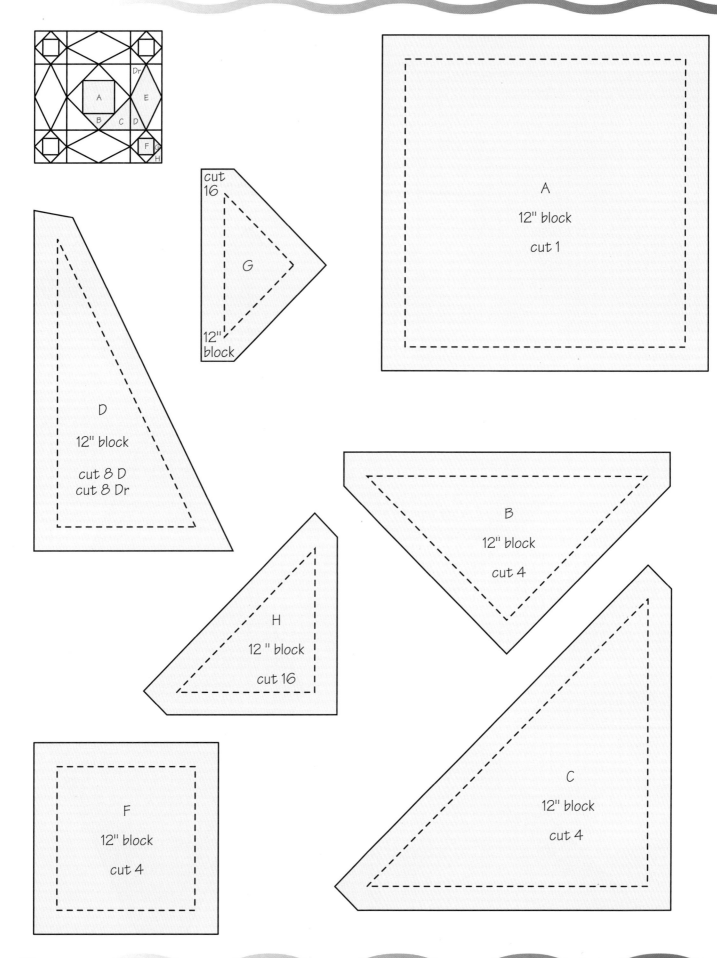

cut
16

G

12"
block

A

12" block

cut 1

D

12" block

cut 8 D
cut 8 Dr

B

12" block

cut 4

H

12 " block

cut 16

C

12" block

cut 4

F

12" block

cut 4

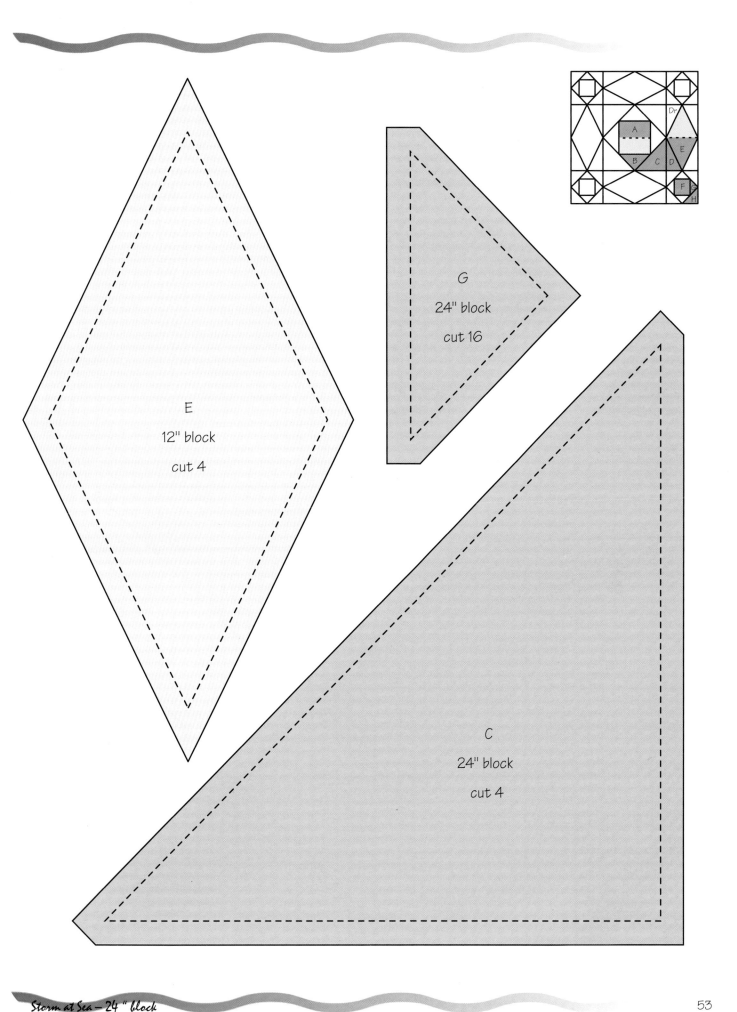

E

12" block

cut 4

G

24" block

cut 16

C

24" block

cut 4

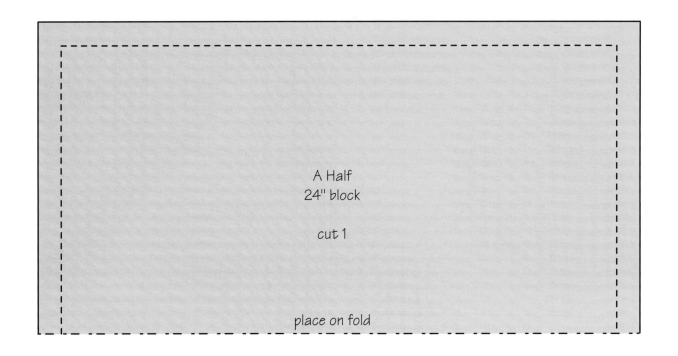

A Half
24" block

cut 1

place on fold

B

24" block

cut 4

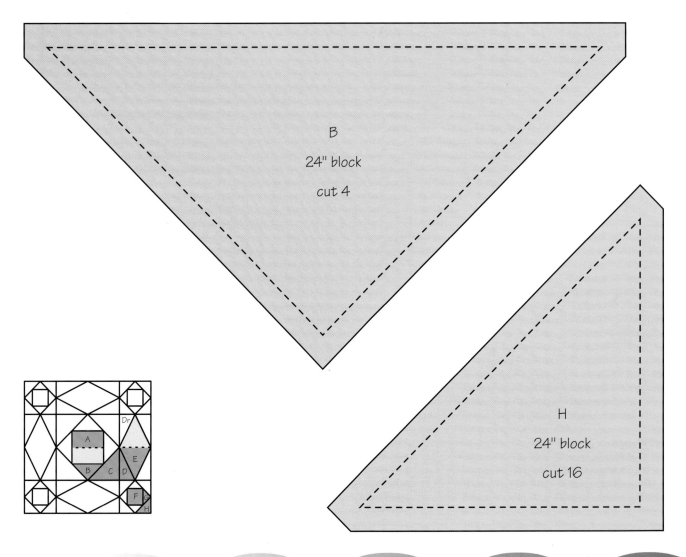

H

24" block

cut 16

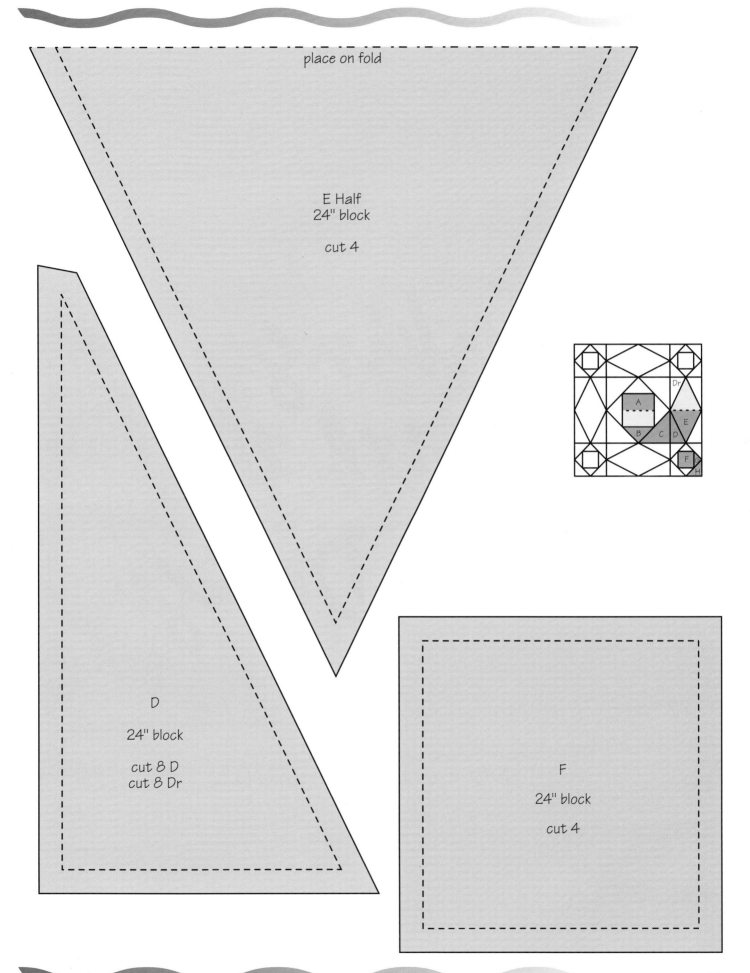

place on fold

E Half
24" block

cut 4

D

24" block

cut 8 D
cut 8 Dr

F

24" block

cut 4

A

Dr

E

B   C   D

F
H

Creating Border Curves

Gwenfai Rees Griffiths

To test various options for border curves, you can paint them on paper and lay them around the quilt top. To achieve a pleasing balanced look, you may want to ask yourself the following questions:

- How wide should the border strips be?
- How wide and deep should the curves be?
- Which colors should be used?

To create curves for a border, first cut the border strips to the appropriate length. Start in the center on the wrong side of the fabric. Place pencil marks in the seam allowances, dividing the border length into segments that correspond with the size of the blocks (Figure 1). In SHADES OF THE SARGASSO SEA, there is one full curve and two half curves for each block.

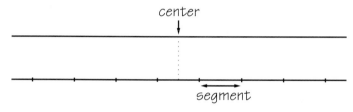

Figure 1. On the wrong side, mark the position for each curve.

Draw a line representing the base of the curve on lightweight cardboard or template plastic. Use a compass or a round object, such as a saucer or plate to draw a curve above the base line. Cut out the curve to use as a template (Figure 2). In SHADES OF THE SARGASSO SEA, two templates were used, and the inner curve is shallower than the outer curve.

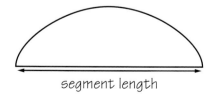

Figure 2. Make a template for the curve.

On the wrong side of the border strip, place the template to fit between the segment marks and trace it with a pencil. Trace all the curves on the border (Figure 3).

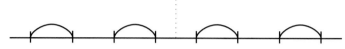

Figure 3. Trace the template on the wrong side of the fabric.

Use the template to draw the curved pieces on a contrasting fabric. Cut the curved fabric pieces, adding ¼" seam allowances by eye as you cut.

Place the pieces right side up on the right side of the border strip and pin. On the wrong side of the border, sew the curves on the pencil line.

Cut away the excess contrasting fabric above the curves, close to the stitching. Cut the border fabric from behind the curved pieces to complete the border.

Sew the border strip to the quilt top, making sure the curves line up with the blocks. The corner curves are formed when the corners are mitered. Gwenfai covered the raw edges of the curves with a bias strip, but decorative stitching could also be used.

Close-up of border section from SHADES OF THE SARGASSO SEA.

Developing Sketches into Quilts

Inge Mardal & Steen Hougs

The theme "Storm at Sea" and the pattern of the corresponding block went with us on vacation to Denmark in the summer of 1998. On the northwestern coast of the country, we photographed and sketched away. We discussed how waves break, how gulls behave, and which palette to apply for rendering the special conditions that signal stormy weather in a seascape. An example of the early sketching is given in Figure 1, which shows a study of gulls over the breakers. Later, we realized that many birds would compete with the other significant elements of the design. We consequently settled for one bird only.

Figure 1. An early sketch for AGAINST THE WIND.

In addition to the photographs and sketches, we brought a multitude of impressions and ideas for the design back to Paris with us. All this made up an ideal base from which to start the implementation of the quilt.

Our objectives were to render the dynamics and kinetic powers of breakers, a monumental stormy sea with foam streaks on massive waves, and to underscore the inherent threat to any mariner who might be out there.

Through a range of sketches, we homed in on the final design. Figure 2 is one of these early layouts in which the final design can be recognized. The physics of breaking waves was studied, and the overall composition was nearly in place.

Pursuing our objectives, we let the background take the

Figure 2. The final design can be recognized in this sketch.

form of a gloomy sky, which builds up with an irresistible determination. We further integrated multiple Storm at Sea patterns as the foundation for the breaking wave, emphasizing the horizontal lines by a gradation in values. These patterns proved ideal for creating a veritable "wall" of approaching water and all its pent-up energy.

Figure 3 shows the first attempt to introduce the Storm at Sea pattern into the final design. As scaled here, the patterns did not sufficiently support the modeling of the breaking wave. They were subsequently scaled down to their final size.

Figure 3. First attempt to introduce the Storm at Sea pattern into the design.

An advantage of the Storm at Sea area appeared to be its inherent regularity. This became clear when a lacy effect was laid diagonally over the field to form the foremost foamy edge of the breaking wave. It provided a highly contrasting value to the foundation of the wave and thereby supported the shaping and modeling of the breaker. The top of the breaking wave was designed in a lively fashion to underscore the release of kinetic energy.

From a design point of view, the gull vertically connects the sky and the sea, avoiding the potential monotony of the horizon. The spray from the breaking wave adds life, spontaneity, and unpredictability to the motif and facilitates the transition from the geometrically stringent quilt blocks to the organic nature of the remaining design.

From the beginning of the project, it was our intention to let the quilting play an active role in achieving our objectives. To facilitate this, the design had to be firm and uncomplicated. To obtain this, we avoided distortion of the Storm at Sea pattern when applying it in the design. Figure 4 shows how the quilting enhances the quilt design. The final design called for paper piecing of the blocks and hand appliquéing the remainder of the work.

Figure 4. The quilting plays an important role in the design.

Blocks to Color

Nancy Lambert

In PATTERNS II (photo on page 20), Nancy used a simple block-to-block setting. Notice that the sashing is part of the block. Make copies of this layout and get out your crayons, colored pencils, or markers to create your own variation of this exquisite quilt.

Medallion Setting

Melinda Myrick Brown

—— Placement of sea urchin insert

Detalied view of GIFT FROM THE SEA by Melinda Myrick Brown.

Quilt assembly

Three different sizes of Storm at Sea blocks (6", 12", and 24") are used to create this medallion-style quilt, which can be made with or without sea urchins (full-sized sea urchin pattern, pages 62–64). Each sea urchin is made from three fabrics. To make templates from the pattern, trace each segment and add ¼" seam allowances all around. The numbers indicate the placement order of the pieces, and the letters are for the colors.

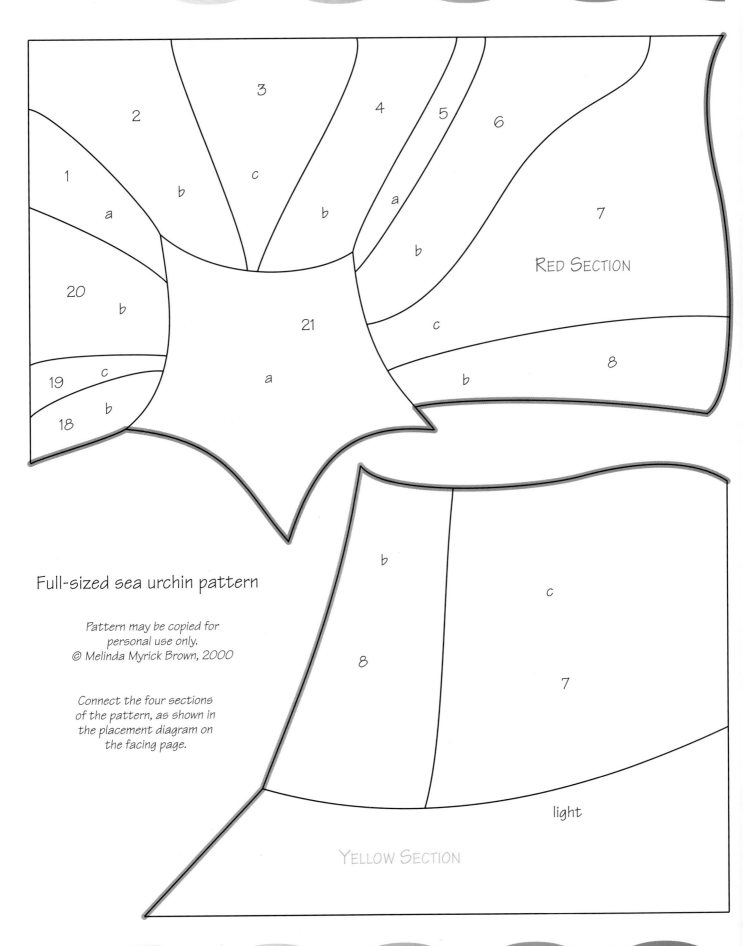

3

2

4

5

6

1

b

c

a

b

7

a

RED SECTION

20

b

b

21

c

19

c

a

8

18

b

b

Full-sized sea urchin pattern

Pattern may be copied for
personal use only.
© Melinda Myrick Brown, 2000

Connect the four sections
of the pattern, as shown in
the placement diagram on
the facing page.

b

c

8

7

light

YELLOW SECTION

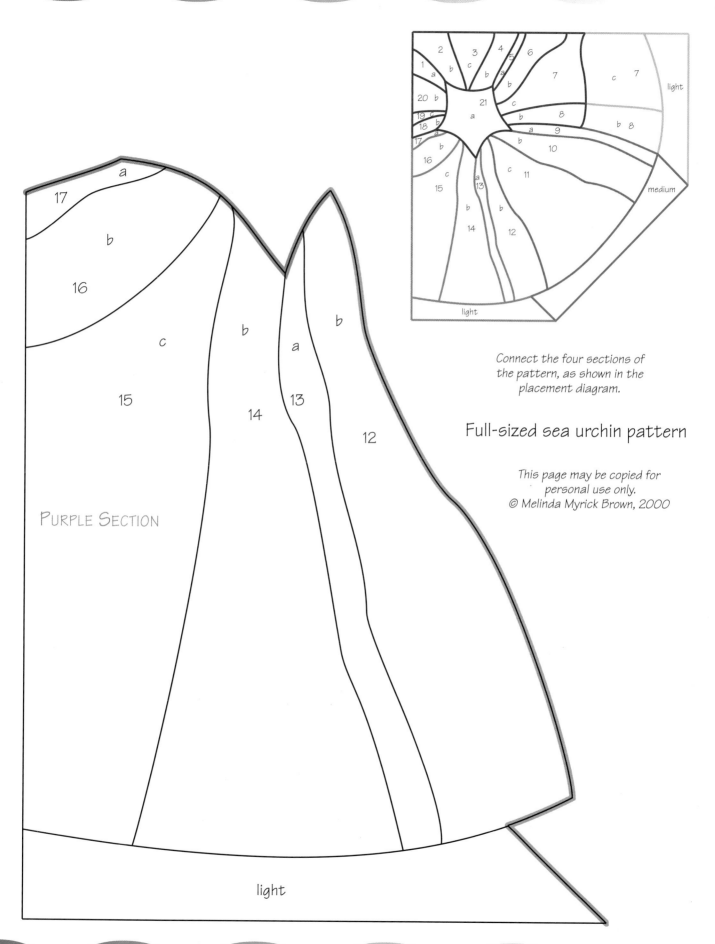

Connect the four sections of the pattern, as shown in the placement diagram.

Full-sized sea urchin pattern

This page may be copied for personal use only.
© Melinda Myrick Brown, 2000

PURPLE SECTION

light

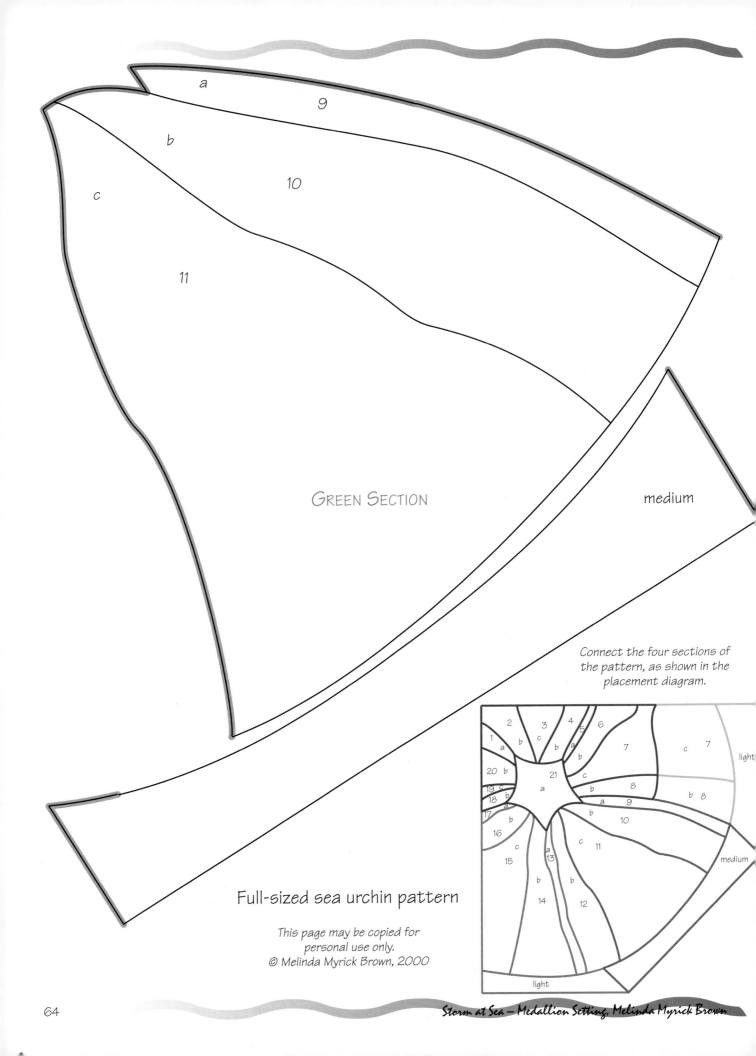

a

9

b

10

c

11

GREEN SECTION

medium

Connect the four sections of
the pattern, as shown in the
placement diagram.

Full-sized sea urchin pattern

This page may be copied for
personal use only.
© Melinda Myrick Brown, 2000

New Designs from Old Favorites

Sherri Bain Driver

Figure 1. Value placement for STORM WARNING.

Draw a "skeleton":

To make a new design based on a traditional block, begin by drawing a skeleton of a quilt made from the block. This can be drawn on a computer or on graph paper. Make several copies and color the different shapes. Changing value placement produces many different designs (Figures 1 – 6). Storm at Sea is especially fun to experiment with because the shapes can be combined many different ways.

You can play with the traditional blocks by subtracting lines from the quilt skeleton. This process can make you aware of shapes you might not have noticed previously. You may end up with really odd shapes, but if you don't mind hand piecing, these quilts can be impressive.

Figure 2. Variation 1.

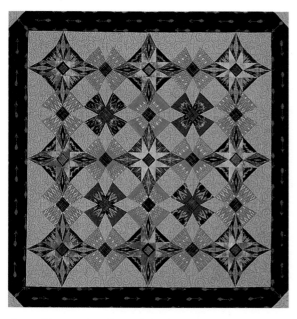

STORM WARNING by Sherri Bain Driver.

Create quilting designs:

Curved quilting lines make a nice complement to the straight piecing lines. For each space that needs a design, you can cut a shape out of paper. Fold the paper in half and cut it snowflake style.

By the time I have shapes that I like, the trash can is full and the floor is littered with snippets of paper, but I am thrilled that I can create my own quilting designs.

Figure 3. Variation 2.

Ikat fabrics

Ikat fabrics have threads with sections that are dyed different colors before the fabric is woven, so the designs appear in the fabric as it is woven. They can be as simple as subtle color changes in a stripe along the weft threads (crosswise grain) of the fabric or as complex as an intricately detailed crane created by dyed sections in both the warp (lengthwise grain) and weft threads. There are many fascinating possibilities lying between these two extremes.

Ikats can be bought from vendors at quilt shows or purchased abroad if you travel to other countries. Clothing made from ikats can be taken apart and cut into pieces for quiltmaking. Because these fabrics are usually hand dyed and hand woven, design repeats are not identical.

Ikats are hard to find and rather expensive, so you will want to buy as much as you can afford when you do find them, and you may have to design a quilt around the yardage purchased. Even though the fabric repeats are not identical, you can still cut nearly identical pieces and place them symmetrically in a block to produce spectacular designs. The number of repeats that can be cut from a piece of fabric dictates its placement in a quilt.

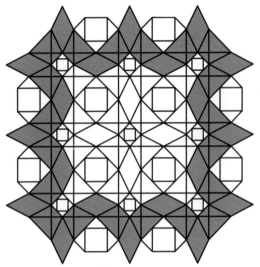

Figure 4. Variation 3.

Figure 5. Variation 4.

Figure 6. Variation 5.

Mer des Sargasses Pattern

Marie Karickhoff

This beautiful quilt can be made from scraps in your stash. The wavy outer border is a variation of the Massachusetts Pieced Border designed by Denyse Saint Arrowman.

Marie altered the original blocks by removing the outer triangles to create a scalloped edge. Then she drafted new corner blocks. Notice that the top and bottom border corners purposely do not match. She also added the perimeter blocks and a solid inner border to create the feelings of airiness and depth.

Referring to the block and sashing diagrams, make the following pieces:
24 main blocks
20 perimeter blocks
4 perimeter corner blocks
110 sash rectangles
63 sash squares

23 border blocks
23 reverse border blocks
2 top border corner blocks
2 bottom border corner blocks

Using the Quilt assembly diagram for placement, sew the pieces together to make the quilt's center. Sew the inner border strips to the four sides of the quilt and miter the corners. Trim off the extra length, leaving a ¼" seam allowance.

MER DES SARGASSES by Marie Karickhoff

Sew 12 border blocks together for the top border and 12 for the bottom border. Sew 13 blocks for each of the side borders. Attach the side borders first, then the top and bottom borders.

Layer and baste the backing, batting, and quilt top. Quilt as desired. MER DES SARGASSES is machine quilted in the ditch around every piece. Use your favorite binding method to finish the raw edges.

FINISHED SIZES
Quilt 66" x 82½" before quilting
Blocks 5½" x 5½"
Sash rectangles 2¾" x 5½"
Sash squares 2¾" x 2¾"

FABRICS
LIGHT SCRAPS EQUAL TO 3⅝ YARDS
96 B, 4 C, 20 D, 20 F, 4 H, 4 Hr, 220 J, 220 Jr, 256 L, 96 M, 146 P, 146 Pr

MEDIUM SCRAPS EQUAL TO 1 YARD
24 A, 63 K, 48 O, 48 Or, 1 Q, 1 Qr

DARK SCRAPS EQUAL TO 3½ YARDS
140 C, 20 E, 4 G, 4 Gr, 110 I, 252 M, 23 N, 23 Nr, 1 Q, 1 Qr, 48 O, 48 Or, 2 P, 2 Pr

INNER BORDER ½ YARD
2 strips 1⅞" x 74"
2 strips 1⅞" x 57½"

BACKING 5 YARDS
2 panels 35½" x 86½"

BINDING ⅝ YARD
10 strips 2" wide

BATTING
72" x 86½"

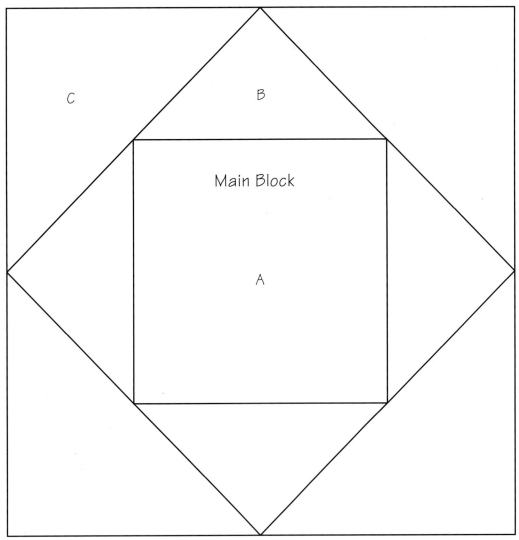

C

B

Main Block

A

Add ¼" seam allowance to
pattern pieces.

Border design adapted from
Massachusetts Pieced Border,
Pieced Border Collection © 1996,
House of White Birches. Pattern
reprinted with permission.

Patterns may be copied for
personal use only.
© Marie Karickhoff, 2000

Quilt assembly diagram

Storm at Sea – MER DES SARGASSES Pattern, Marie Karickhoff

Border design adapted from Massachusetts Pieced Border, Pieced Border Collection © 1996, House of White Birches. Pattern reprinted with permission.

Patterns may be copied for personal use only.
© Marie Karickhoff, 2000

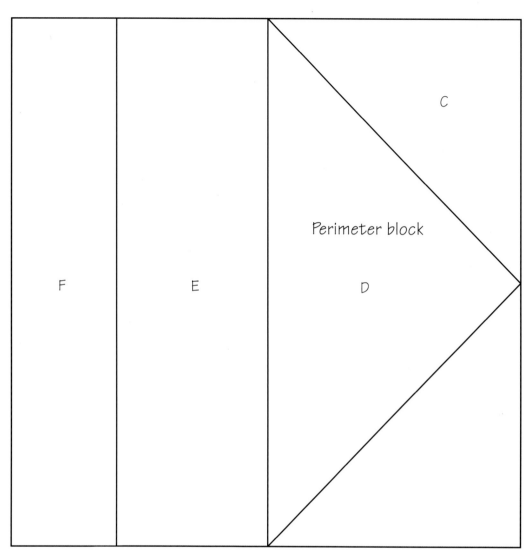

F

E

Perimeter block

D

C

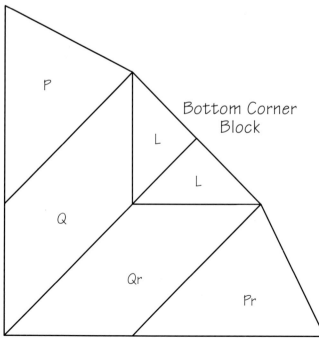

P

Bottom Corner Block

L

L

Q

Qr

Pr

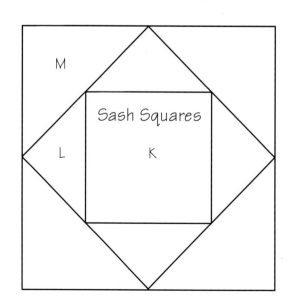

M

Sash Squares

L

K

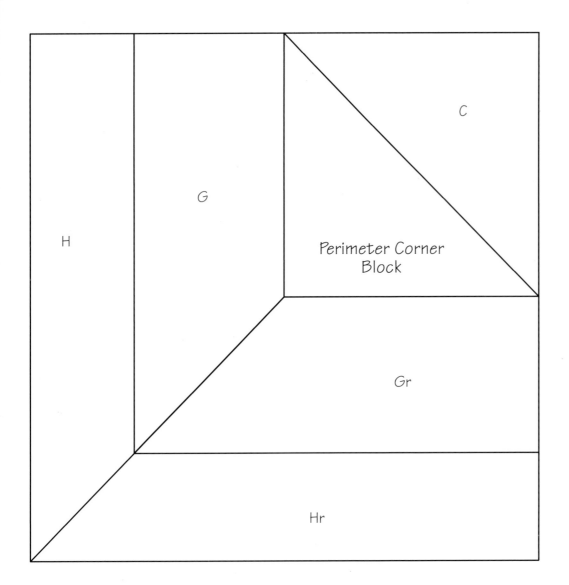

C

G

H

Perimeter Corner
Block

Gr

Hr

Add ¼" seam allowance to
pattern pieces.

Border design adapted from
Massachusetts Pieced Border,
Pieced Border Collection © 1996,
House of White Birches. Pattern
reprinted with permission.

Patterns may be copied for
personal use only.
© Marie Karickhoff, 2000

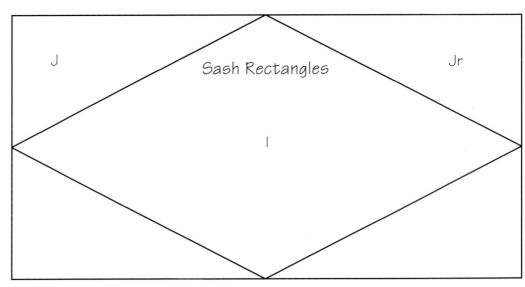

J

Jr

Sash Rectangles

I

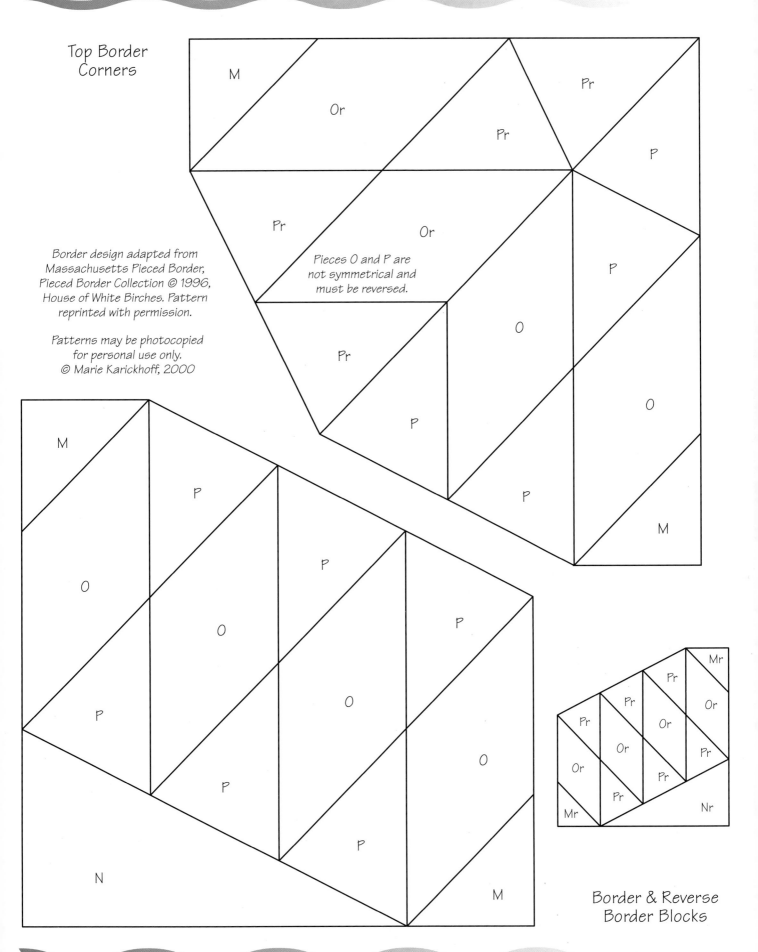

Top Border
Corners

M

Or

Pr

Pr

P

Pr

Or

Pieces O and P are
not symmetrical and
must be reversed.

P

Pr

O

P

O

Border design adapted from
Massachusetts Pieced Border,
Pieced Border Collection © 1996,
House of White Birches. Pattern
reprinted with permission.

Patterns may be photocopied
for personal use only.
© Marie Karickhoff, 2000

P

P

M

M

P

O

P

P

P

O

O

P

P

P

N

M

Mr

Pr

Pr

Or

Or

Pr

Or

Or

Pr

Pr

Mr

Pr

Nr

Border & Reverse
Border Blocks

Storm at Sea Block Variation

Yoshiko Kobayashi

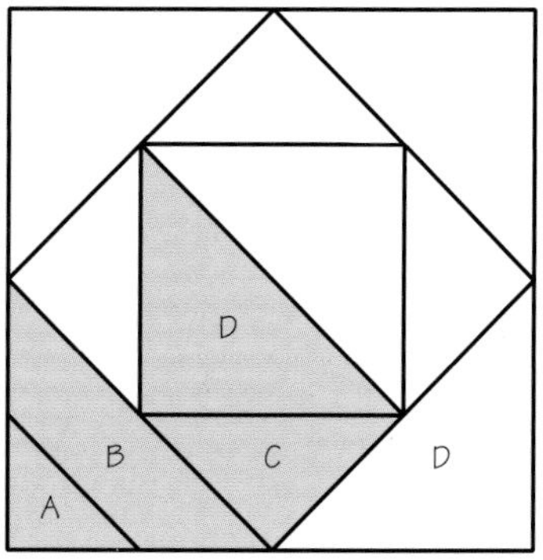

Yoshiko has created a new design by subdividing the patches in a traditional Storm at Sea block. Her original drawing of ANCIENT MIRROR CAME FROM ACROSS THE SEA, on page 74, shows how she developed her block variations into a spectacular quilt. Mix and match the block sections to create your own blocks and quilt designs.

9½" Block

Full-sized patterns

D

C

B

A

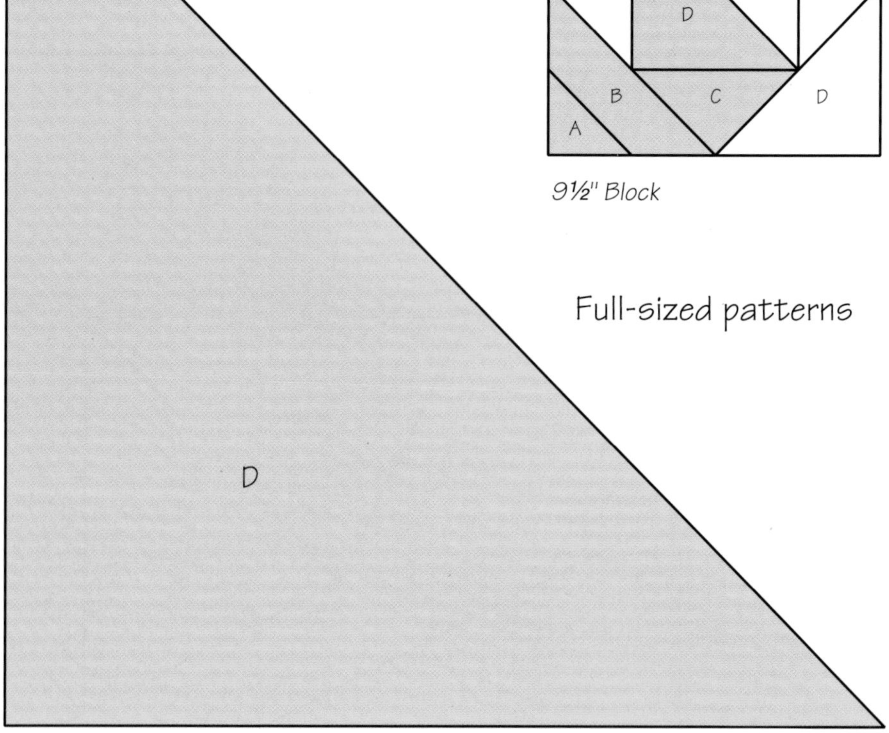

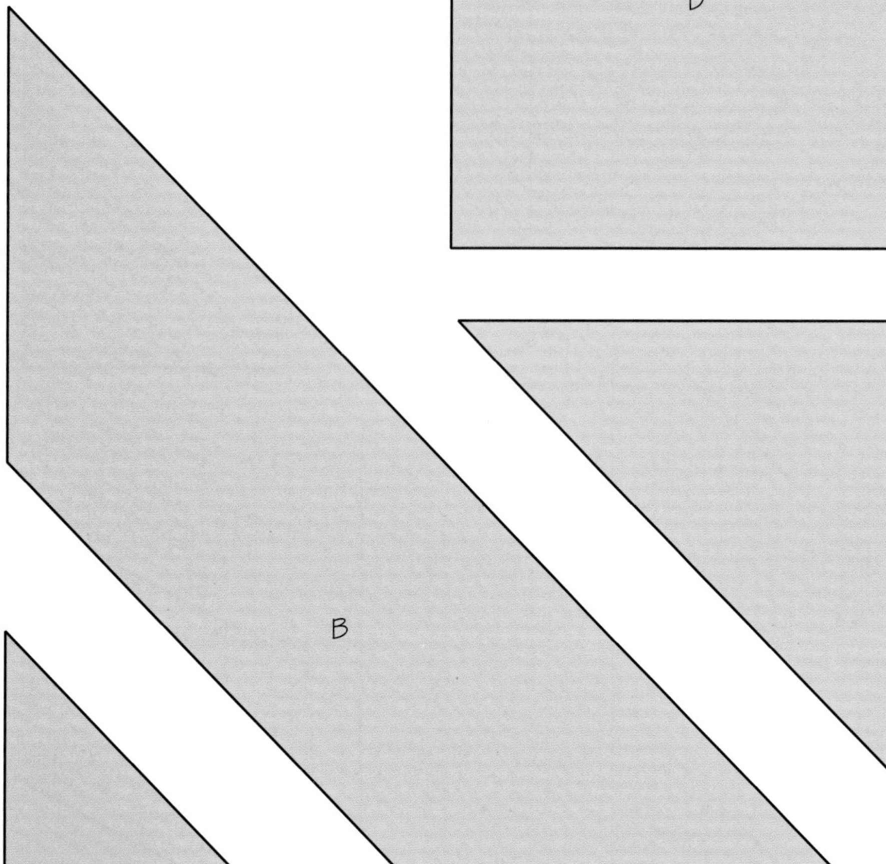

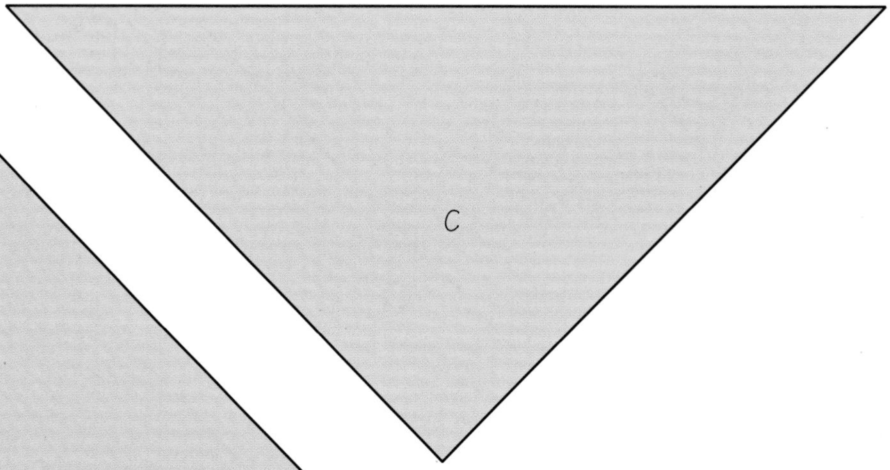

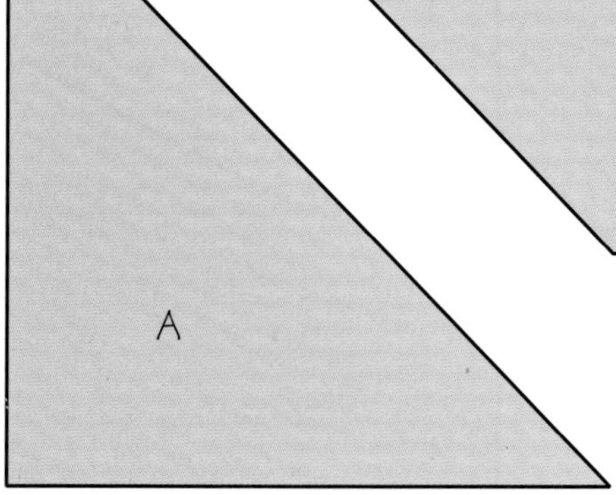

Add ¼" seam allowance to pattern pieces.

Patterns may be copied for personal use only.
© Yoshiko Kobayashi, 2000

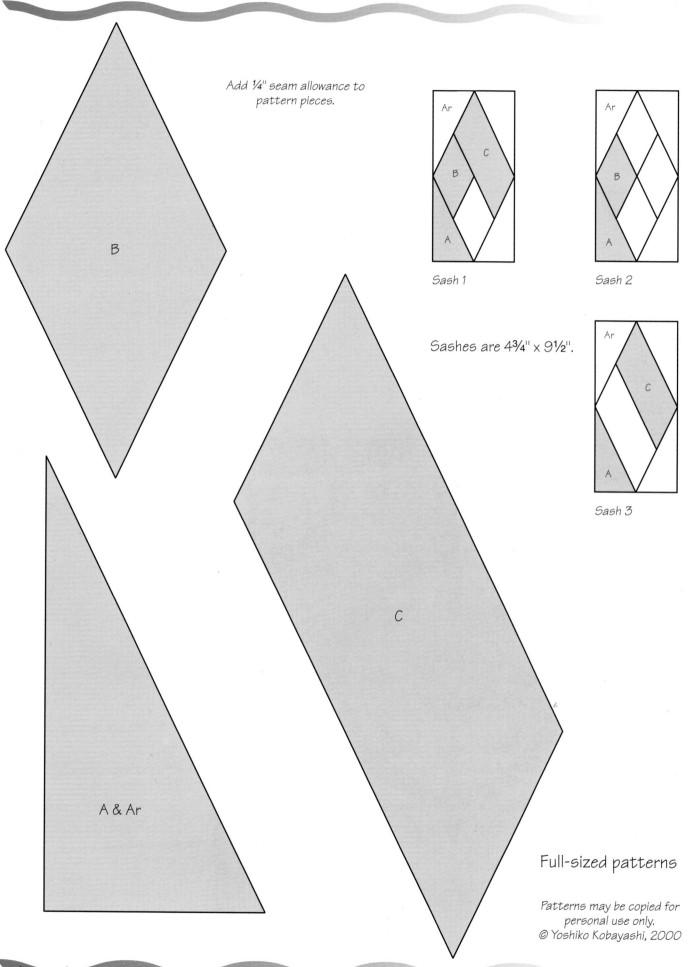

Add ¼" seam allowance to pattern pieces.

B

Ar
C
B
A

Sash 1

Ar
B
A

Sash 2

Sashes are 4¾" x 9½".

Ar
C
A

Sash 3

A & Ar

C

Full-sized patterns

Patterns may be copied for personal use only.
© Yoshiko Kobayashi, 2000

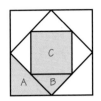

4¾" Block

4¾" Block

Full-sized patterns

Add ¼" seam allowance to pattern pieces.

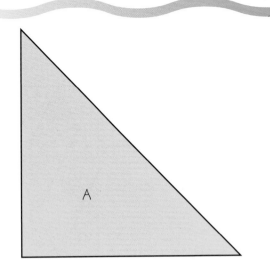

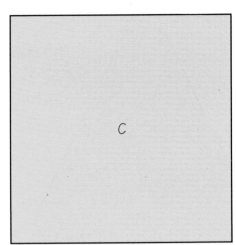

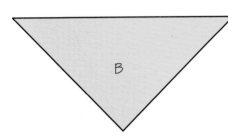

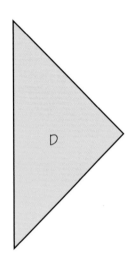

Yoshiko's original drawing of ANCIENT MIRROR CAME FROM ACROSS THE SEA.

Storm at Sea – Storm at Sea Block Variation, Yoshiko Kobayashi

Seiryu, the blue dragon from the east.

Quilting pattern

ANCIENT MIRROR CAME FROM ACROSS THE SEA
by Yoshiko Kobayashi.

Suzaku, the red phoenix from the south.

Quilting pattern

Large Block Overlay

Peggy Luey

To design a quilt with a large transparent block like REQUIEM AT SEA, you will need to have the same number of blocks in your quilt as there are grid divisions in one block. For instance, the Storm at Sea block is drafted on a four-by-four grid, so you will need to make 16 blocks for your quilt (Figure 1).

You can draft the whole quilt, full-size, if you want, but just a quarter of the quilt can give you all the templates for the patches. Draft four full-size blocks and tape them together to create one fourth of the quilt. Then, using the "seams" between the blocks as grid lines, draft one fourth of one large block on top (Figure 2). Choosing fabrics with slightly darker values for the overlying block will help to create that transparent feeling.

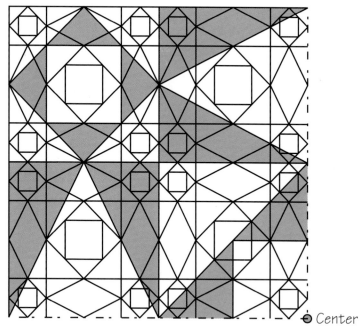

Figure 2. Drawing of one-fourth of quilt, showing the overlying transparent block.

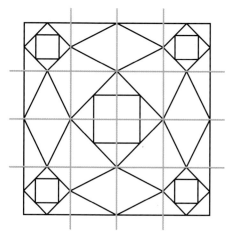

Figure 1. The Storm at Sea block is constructed on a four-by-four grid, creating 16 divisions.

REQUIEM AT SEA by Peggy Luey.

Appliquéd Whale

Sharon Malec

The whale can be appliquéd as a unit before being appliquéd to the background. Reduce or enlarge the pattern as needed for your project and use it for appliqué, quilting, or embroidery.

FABRIC REQUIREMENTS
1 yard blue background
½ yard blue-gray for whale
3 or 4 fat quarters of blues for waves

Making templates

Enlarge the whale pattern to the desired size on a photocopier to use as a master pattern. The size used in WHALE OF A STORM was 34½" x 24". Trace pieces 1–16 on the dull side of a sheet of freezer paper. Number the pieces and mark all the registration points. Cut the freezer paper pieces apart to use as templates for the appliqué.

Cutting fabric

Select the desired fabrics. Press the pattern piece to the right side of your chosen fabric with a hot iron. With the paper pattern in place, cut out the fabric piece, including approximately ½" for a turn-under allowance beyond the edges of the paper. If you want to preview the fabric, remove the freezer paper and pin the fabric piece to the corresponding area of the master pattern. Press the freezer paper pattern back in place before proceeding to next step.

Appliquéing whale

Referring to the Assembly Order, begin with pieces 6 and 7. Keep the freezer paper in place and leave the edges of the first piece unturned.

Hold the second piece between your fingers and gently turn the allowance to the wrong side, using the paper pattern as a guide. When the edge is turned, press lightly with an iron.

To join it to the first piece, apply a glue stick to the allowance on the right side of the first piece, as needed. Using the registration marks, align the pieces and press them in place with your fingers or an iron.

Continue adding pieces in this manner. When all the pieces have been joined, turn all the outside edges before removing the freezer paper pattern. Place the completed whale on the background, lift the edges slightly, and apply a glue stick to attach the unit to the background. Appliqué the outer edges.

ASSEMBLY ORDER

WHALE
Unit 1: join pieces 6 and 7.
Unit 2: join pieces 1, 2, then 5.
Unit 3: join pieces 3 and 4.
Join all three units to complete the whale.

WAVES
Unit 1: join pieces 9 and 10, add 11, 12, 13, then 8.
Unit 2: join pieces 14 and 15, add 16.
Join the units.

Using monofilament or matching thread, machine appliqué the finished piece to the background with a small zigzag stitch.

Quilting the medallion

The medallion can be joined to plain borders or to Storm at Sea blocks. Using free-motion machine quilting, add water section to the whale's tail with white thread. Stitching can be enhanced with cheesecloth or fabric paints.

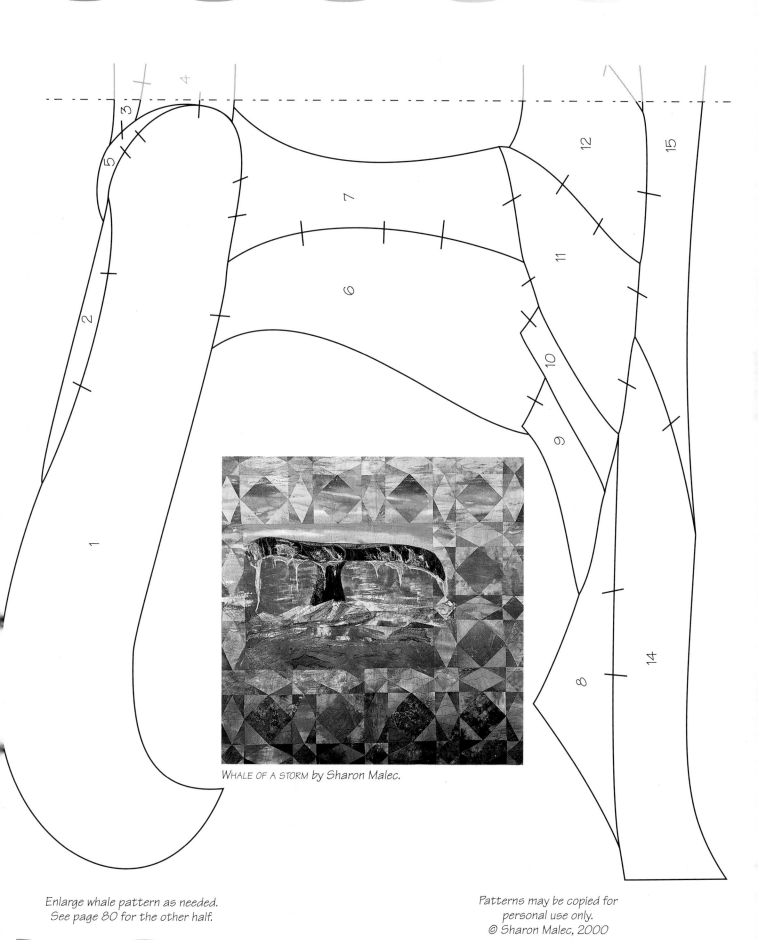

WHALE OF A STORM by Sharon Malec.

Enlarge whale pattern as needed.
See page 80 for the other half.

Patterns may be copied for
personal use only.
© Sharon Malec, 2000

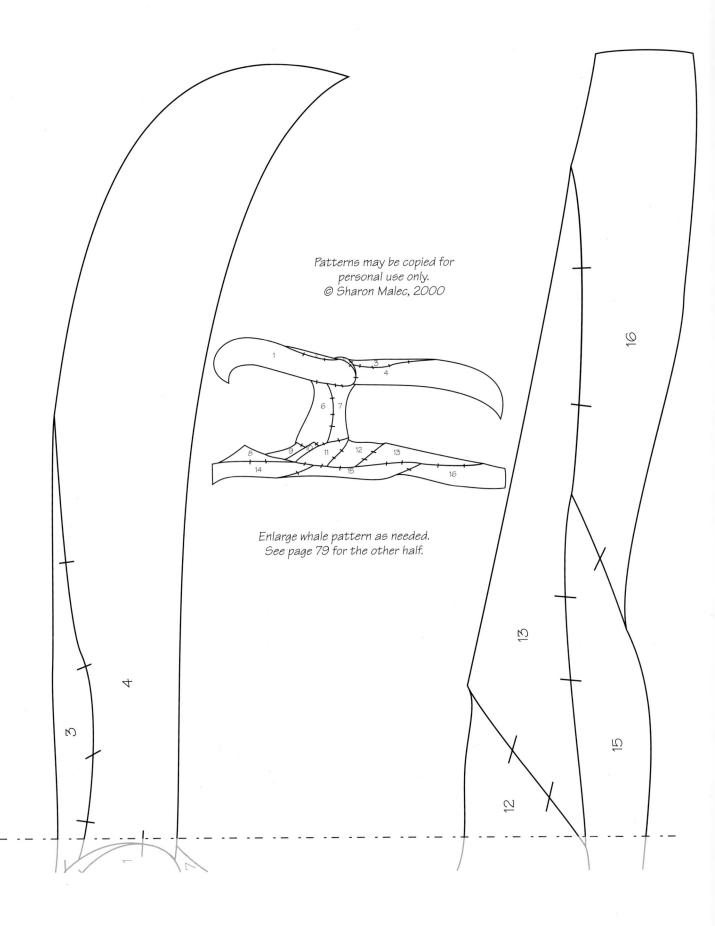

Patterns may be copied for
personal use only.
© Sharon Malec, 2000

Enlarge whale pattern as needed.
See page 79 for the other half.

I was quite apprehensive about transferring the image of the women to the quilt because I could see, in my mind's eye, how they should look. No technique that I had ever used was going to work. The most valuable tool turned out to be a photocopying machine. Who would have guessed the copy machine that I had considered a slightly frivolous purchase would become one of my most valuable quilting tools?

Using a news photo that showed a group of refugees, I drew three faces and bodies, simplifying them until they were just a few lines that still conveyed emotion and personality. With the copy machine, I enlarged them to the size needed and printed multiple copies of each woman.

I arranged the drawings on my design wall, overlapping them. The one that was the most expressive was placed in the most prominent position. I glued them together in this arrangement and called this my master drawing. Then, several large sheets of tracing paper were taped together and pinned on top of the master drawing. With a permanent marker, I traced the master drawing on the tracing paper, marking where every piece would fit in, just as would be done for an appliqué project.

I placed the entire arrangement on top of a piece of muslin, cut large enough to accommodate the ladies. All three layers were pinned to my pinnable cutting board, but the two sides of the tracing paper were left unpinned so that appliqué pieces could be placed underneath.

I cut tiny scraps of paisleys and other fabrics and glued them to each section of the tracing paper to use as a "map" so I wouldn't get lost. As I worked, I placed another piece of tracing paper over each section and traced it. This tracing was cut apart so the pieces could be used as patterns for cutting the fabrics. I then cut each pattern from the chosen fabric and slipped this piece under the tracing paper map. As each piece was placed, it was glued to the muslin backing with a glue stick. When all the pieces were accounted for, except the faces and hands, the tracing paper map was removed, and the pieces were satin stitched with black thread.

I ironed a double-faced fusible to the back of the beige paisley fabric for the faces and hands and cut this fabric into 8½" x 11" sheets. Using the original drawings, I printed the faces and hands with the copy machine on the beige paisley and used a hot iron to set the toner on the fabric. I removed the backing from the fusible, placed the faces and hands where I wanted them, ironed them down, and satin stitched the edges.

To quilt the women, I stitched around their facial features and the paisley designs in the skin to integrate everything and make the pieces seem embroidered. Amazingly enough, the women looked just as I had envisioned them.

Here are some of the elongated blocks used in KOSOVO – A WORLD IN FLAMES for you to play with and perhaps add to a project.

...as I was rearranging my longest blocks on the design wall, I noticed that... these blocks could look like flames.

Elongated Block

Claudia used various sizes of elongated blocks in her quilt. Here is one for you to play with. Trace each lettered patch and add ¼" seam allowances when cutting the fabric pieces.

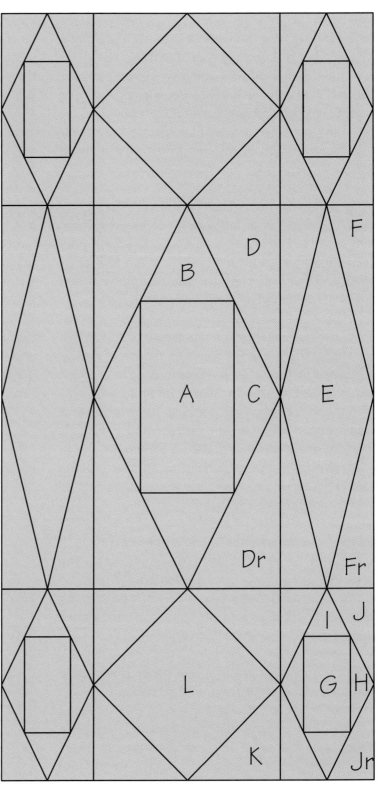

Detailed view of the different size Storm at Sea blocks Myers used in KOSOVO – A WORLD OF FLAMES.

Maurine embroidered leaves on her Storm at Sea quilt. You can add these leaf patterns to your own quilt design or take a walk through your neighborhood to collect leaves for tracing. Patterns for two of the elongated blocks from AUTUMN LEAVES (photo on page 38) are given on page 84.

Appliqué, embroidery, or quilting patterns

Detailed view of the different leaves Maurine used in AUTUMN LEAVES.

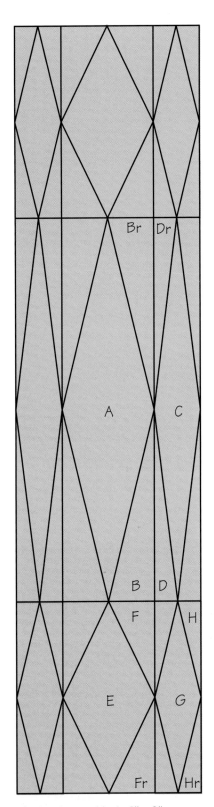

AUTUMN LEAVES block, 2" x 8".

Trace each lettered patch and add ¼" seam allowances when cutting the fabric pieces.

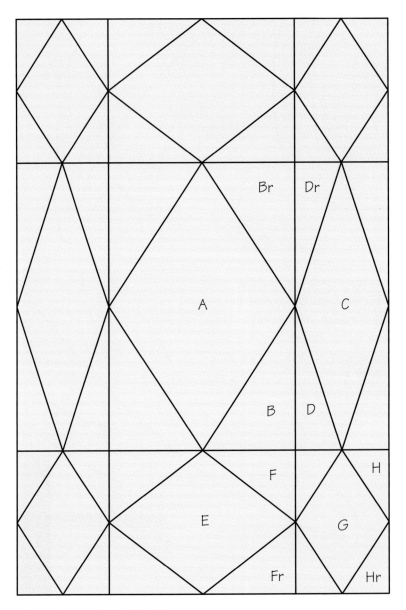

AUTUMN LEAVES block, 4" x 6".

Slanted Block

Judy Sogn

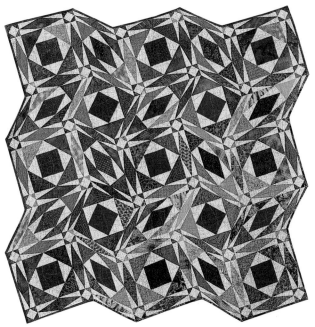

Front view of STORM AT ...GULP...SEASICK *by Judy Sogn.*

Judy carried the "Storm at Sea" theme to the back of her quilt with a variation of the Snail's Trail block. Try your hand at making some slanted blocks. Patch patterns are on pages 86–88.

Back view of STORM AT ...GULP...SEASICK *by Judy Sogn.*

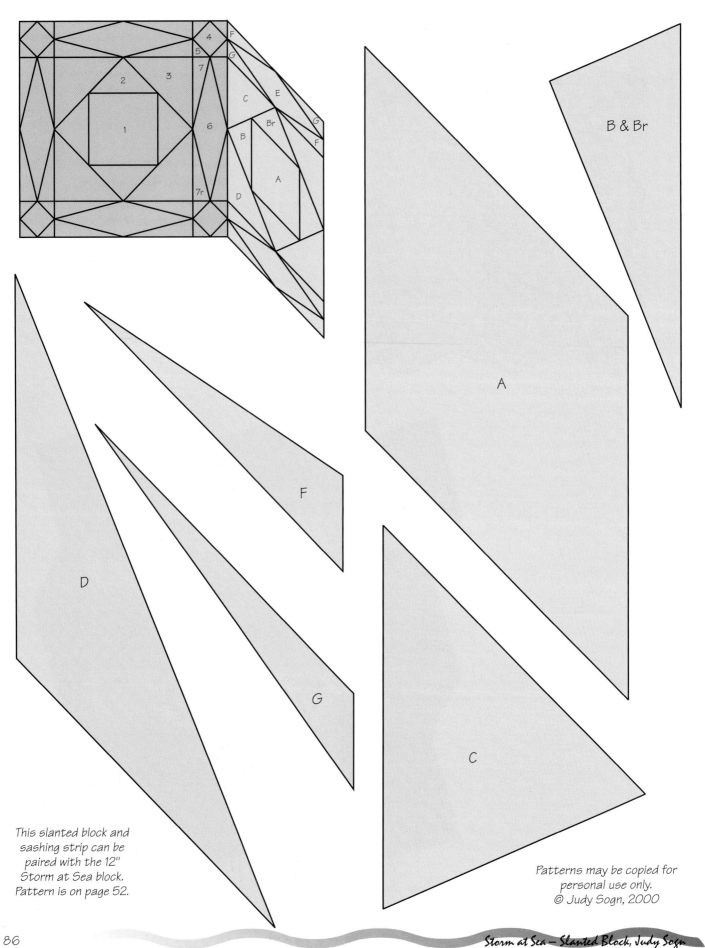

This slanted block and sashing strip can be paired with the 12" Storm at Sea block. Pattern is on page 52.

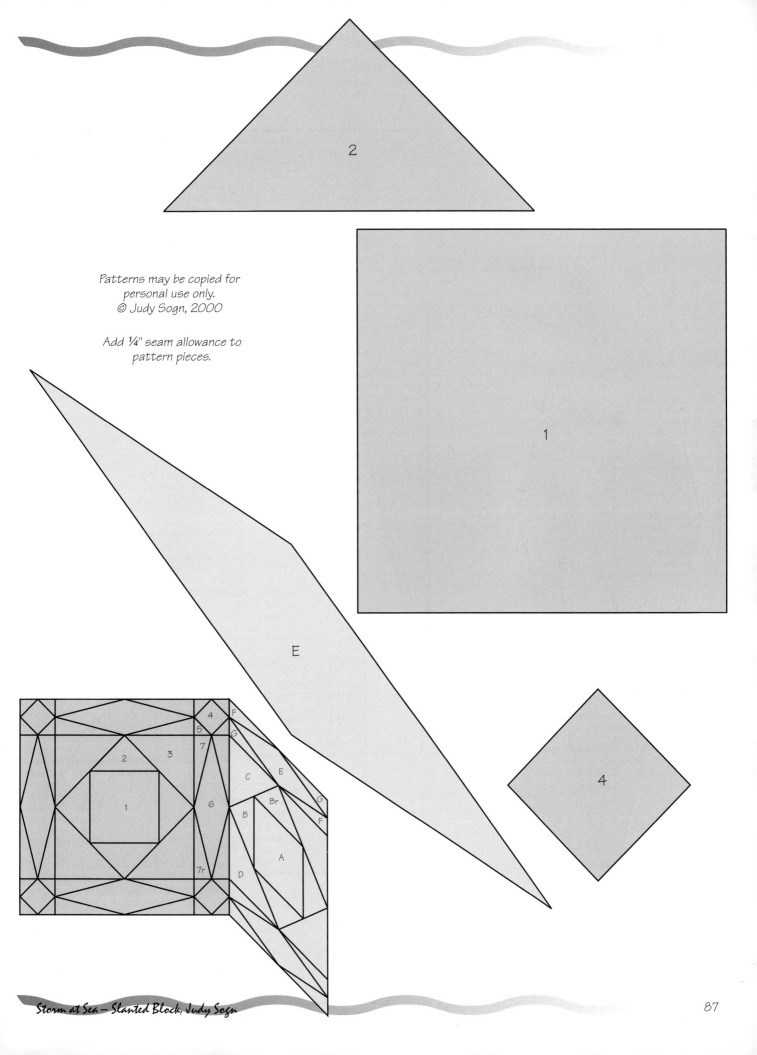

2

Patterns may be copied for
personal use only.
© Judy Sogn, 2000

Add ¼" seam allowance to
pattern pieces.

1

E

4

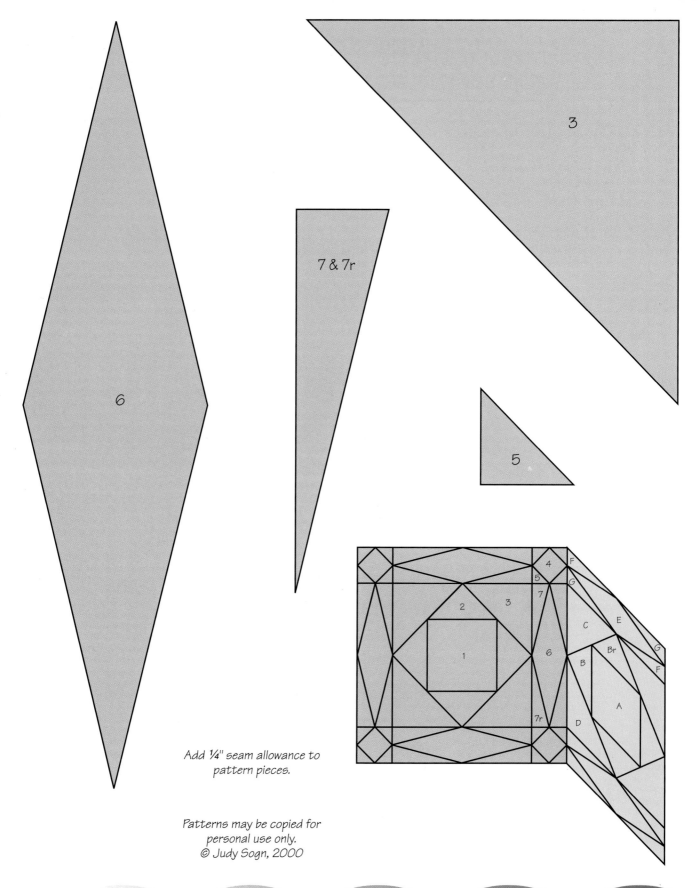

6

3

7 & 7r

5

4
5
F
G
2
3
7
C
E
1
6
Br
B
G
F
A
7r
D

Add ¼" seam allowance to
pattern pieces.

Patterns may be copied for
personal use only.
© Judy Sogn, 2000

Tumbling Diamonds
Claire Anne Teagan

TUMBLING SEAS was made with paper foundation piecing. If you use a photocopier to make the foundations, be sure to check for distortion by comparing the copies to the original patterns in the book.

Cut the foundations on the outside lines. The foundations do not have seam allowances, so you will need to allow extra fabric when sewing and trimming the units.

Use a size 12 or 14 needle, which will make holes large enough to tear the paper off easily. Set the stitch length shorter than usual (about 1.5 on many machines) to keep the stitches from pulling out when the paper is removed.

Sew the fabrics to the foundations in numerical order. Trim each seam to ¼" as it is sewn, press the seam to set the stitches, then press the seam allowances open. You will need to make four of each unit for each of the 12 diamonds.

TUMBLING SEAS by Claire Anne Teagan.

Original colored drawing for TUMBLING SEAS.

Trim the units, leaving a ¼" seam allowance around the edges. Sew the units together to make the diamonds. Before the paper is removed, twill tape can be sewn around the outside of the diamonds to stabilize the bias edges.

Sew the light- and medium-color diamonds together to form an eight-pointed star, then set in the darker diamonds around the outside of the star.

For the corner triangles, cut two 16½" rectangles in half diagonally. Sew the oversized triangles to the quilt, then trim them, leaving a ¼" allowance beyond the points of the hexagon.

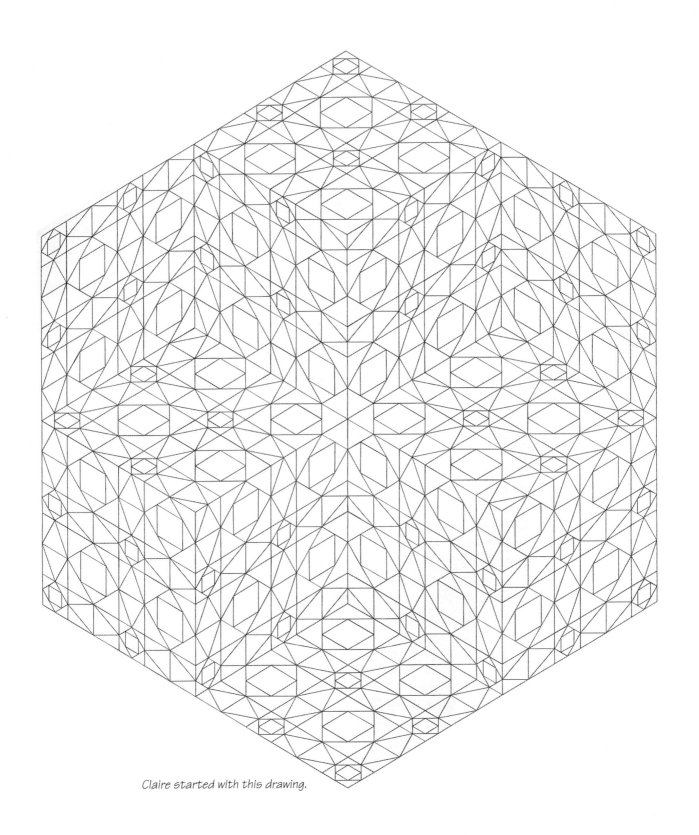

Claire started with this drawing.

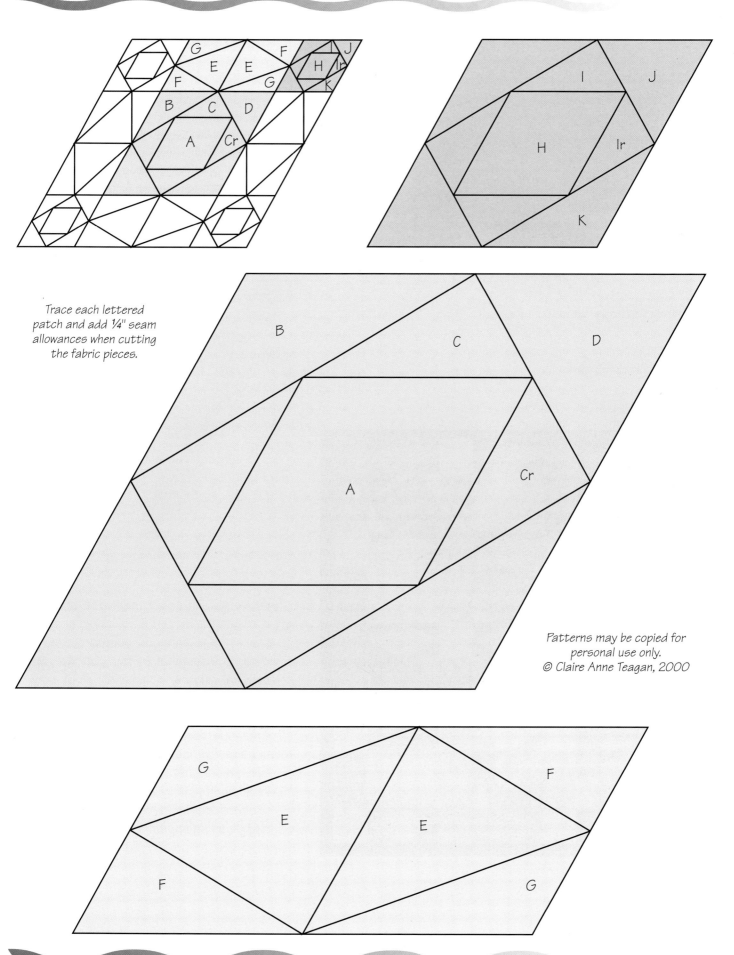

Trace each lettered
patch and add ¼" seam
allowances when cutting
the fabric pieces.

Patterns may be copied for
personal use only.
© Claire Anne Teagan, 2000

Medallion Setting
Adrienne Yorinks

I always start a new quilt with a quick note showing the basic idea and what's most important about the piece. It is one of my favorite parts of creating a new design, and it can be just an idea, a title, a feeling, or a sketch. Rarely is the first design exactly what happens in the completed quilt, but there are always elements that remain.

I find it helpful to return to the original impetus of a work at various times while making a quilt. Many times, although it is a part of the quilt in some form, it is no longer the most important part. The way I work is more improvisational in construction, and when one works that way, the quilt itself begins to have a voice in the quiltmaking process.

Adrienne starts with a quick sketch, defining the design features she wants to consider emphasizing.

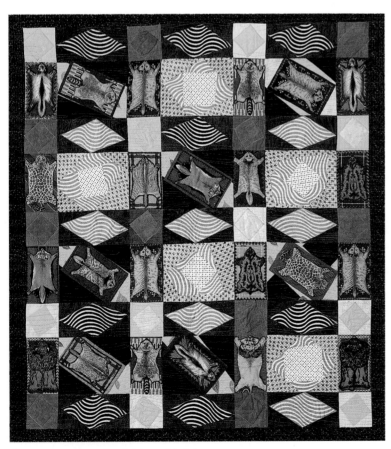

DUCKING THE STORM by Adrienne Yorinks.

What was most fun about making DUCKING THE STORM was incorporating the vintage tobacco company premiums. It is typical of my work to use unusual fabrics, either vintage or contemporary, and they are truly what makes creating quilts challenging and fun. I encourage readers to look for unusual fabrics. Many times, they may seem more difficult to use at first, but in actuality, they can really make the process easier by creating a strong and pleasing impact immediately.

A dream long held by American Quilter's Society founders Bill and Meredith Schroeder and by quilters worldwide was realized on April 25, 1991, when the Museum of the American Quilter's Society (MAQS, pronounced "Max") opened its doors in Paducah, Kentucky. As is stated in brass lettering over the building's entrance, this national non-profit institution is dedicated to "honoring today's quilter" by stimulating and supporting the study, appreciation, and development of quiltmaking throughout the world.

The 27,000 square-foot facility includes a center exhibition gallery, featuring a selection of the 184 quilts by today's quiltmakers comprising the Schroeder/MAQS Collection and two additional galleries displaying exhibits of antique and other contemporary quilts. Lectures, workshops, and other related activities are held on the site in spacious modern classrooms. A gift and book shop makes available a wide selection of fine crafts and more than 400 quilt and textile books. The museum is open all year, Monday through Saturday, and is wheelchair accessible.

For more information, write MAQS, P.O. Box 1540, Paducah, KY 42002-1540, phone: 270-442-8856, or e-mail: maqsmus@apex.net.

The Quiltmakers

The Quilts

This is only a small selection of the books available from the
AMERICAN QUILTER'S SOCIETY.
AQS books are known worldwide for timely topics, clear writing,
beautiful color photos, and accurate illustrations and patterns.
The following books are available from your local bookseller,
quilt shop, or public library.

#5176 $24.95

#5098 $16.95

#4911 $16.95

#4995 $19.95

#5591 $19.95

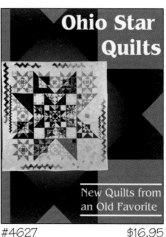

#4627 $16.95

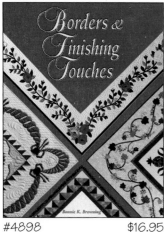

#4898 $16.95

#5296 $16.95

#4918 $16.95

Look for these books nationally or call 1-800-626-5420